Itanium Rising
Breaking Through Moore's
Second Law of Computing Power

D1553626

ISBN 013046415-5

90000

9 780130 464156

HEWLETT-PACKARD PRESS STRATEGIC BOOKS

Itanium Rising
Breaking Through Moore's
Second Law of Computing Power

Jim Carlson
Jerry Huck

Prentice Hall PTR
Upper Saddle River, New Jersey 07458
www.phptr.com

Library of Congress Cataloging-in-Publication Data

CIP data available.

Editorial/production supervision: *Mary Sudul*
Acquisitions editor: *Jill Harry*
Manufacturing manager: *Alexis R. Heydt*
Composition: *FASTpages*
Marketing manager: *Dan DePasquale*
Cover design: *Anthony Gemmellaro*
Cover design direction: *Jerry Votta*
Editorial assistant: *Katie Wolf*

Publisher, Hewlett-Packard Books: *Patricia Pekary*

Published by Prentice Hall PTR
Prentice-Hall, Inc.
Upper Saddle River, New Jersey 07458

Prentice Hall books are widely used by corporations and government agencies for training, marketing, and resale.
The publisher offers discounts on this book when ordered in bulk quantities. For more information, contact Corporate Sales Department, Phone: 800-382-3419; FAX: 201-236-7141; E-mail: corpsales@prenhall.com
Or write: Prentice Hall PTR, Corporate Sales Dept., One Lake Street, Upper Saddle River, NJ 07458.

Printed in the United States of America
10   9   8   7   6   5   4   3

ISBN 0-13-046415-5

Pearson Education LTD.
Pearson Education Australia PTY, Limited
Pearson Education Singapore, Pte. Ltd.
Pearson Education North Asia Ltd.
Pearson Education Canada, Ltd.
Pearson Educación de Mexico, S.A. de C.V.
Pearson Education — Japan
Pearson Education Malaysia, Pte. Ltd.

Contents

v

Foreword

Richard A. DeMillo,
Vice President of Technology Strategy, Hewlett-Packard Company

The commercial success of technologies is always as much about sociology and economics as it is about physics and engineering. The pitch of a machine screw seems like a humble comparison to modern microprocessor technology, but a standard way to measure screw pitch meant that 19th century machine designers could concentrate on larger issues, such as power and efficiency. The wealth of the industrialized world in the 21st century owes much to a humble industry standard. Wherever there is a "golden age" in the build-out of an industry, standards and standard components play a key role. They allow innovative companies to flourish by adding value to the standard that will be recognized and rewarded in the marketplace. Competitors are doomed to invest in both value-added capabilities and proprietary components and interfaces but are rewarded only for the added value. In the early 1990s several computer companies, including Hewlett-Packard, began to consider whether the IT industry might not also benefit from industry-standard components.

Microprocessors are different from machine screws in one major respect. Unlike components that do not change much from one generation to the next, microprocessors double their performance every 18 months, following the law attributed to Gordon Moore. Therefore, any company that continues to invest in a proprietary microprocessor has to sustain or increase that investment just to stay on the "technology curve."

Although it was unforeseen in 1990, the value side of the equation is today driven by ubiquitous Internet services. Utility and grid computing, Web services, rich media applications, asset utilization, service management, security, availability, connectivity, and lower cost of ownership are some examples of value drivers that today seem to be following their own exponential growth curves. In the eyes of the customer, innovation in these areas is meaningful, even as the underlying computing and communications infrastructure fade into the background.

This is the context for the introduction of Intel's Itanium processor family, a new 64-bit series of microprocessors based on the IA-64 architecture co-developed by HP and Intel. Whole families of new services ranging from Internet-based voice/ data services for mobile workers using handheld devices to resilient, dependable, mission-critical enterprise infrastructure will be accelerated by next-generation 64-bit processors. But an industry-standard processor will be the only one with volumes sufficient to sustain truly differentiated prices when compared with proprietary processor designs.

The IA-64 technology began in HP Labs but evolved into a collaborative effort with Intel to become real. The technology itself is a tripod that rests on the architectural definition, the processor chip, and the compiler. It is a technology at the beginning of its life and so will improve as it moves along the maturity curve. The architecture lends itself to improvement. The EPIC architecture, on which the Intel Itanium processor family is based, allows for continual improvement by compiler software. This architecture has, so to speak, headroom. An investment in Itanium today will put developers and customers alike on a growth path that extends to the foreseeable future.

The Intel Itanium processor family is about the future, but it is a very real technology. Even in the very early days of its use, there were hundreds of systems running in R&D labs. It has architectural features that make it the compelling choice for many high-volume applications. The Itanium processor family protection-ring architecture and native speed on arithmetic, for example, means that Itanium is today the world's highest performance open, secure processor. It runs HP-UX, Linux, and Windows with hundreds of popular applications.

Rarely have companies seen as clearly into the future as HP and Intel did when they undertook the development of the technology that we today see as the Itanium processor family.

Introduction

Why You Need to Know About the Intel Itanium Processor Family

When you think of the business pressures that influence technical innovation and microprocessor design, several drivers come to mind immediately. Processor speed. Scalability. Cross-platform compatibility. Seamless transitions from legacy hardware and software. Reliability at a level that eliminates downtime. And perhaps the biggest driver of all today: the nebulous concepts involving Internet computing and its resulting effect on electronic business.

The Demands of Change

As little as 20 years ago, the capabilities—and problems—resulting from vast numbers of machines that collected and collated data simply did not exist. Information storage and retrieval was primitive and expensive. The ability to share data between machines was limited by the current day's wiring standards and architecture. The entire field of IT industry players, from the massive wafer fabrication plants to the startup dotcom operating out of your neighbor's garage were barely out of their infancy.

There has been a lot of change since then. Some of the key developments resulting from the incredible speed of development in the industry include:

- The need for computers to handle ever-more complex data and computations.
- Vast improvement of tracking and storing customer information.

- The accumulation of vast amounts of data resulting from the proliferation of data in digital format and the ease of creating new content and distributing online.
- Resulting need to analyze and mine this data for only the most relevant parts.
- The need to squeeze ever-more processing power out of the IT investment—to handle today's complex software, higher user demands, and all of the aforementioned tasks.

To these resulting demands, I would add two more:

- The recognition of Reduced Instruction Set Computing (RISC)'s limitations in today's world.
- Developing the idea of computing as a service, not a hardware- or software-dependent model.

The Intel Itanium Processor Family

The Intel Itanium[1] architecture was, in essence, designed to meet all of these challenges and take corporate IT services to the next level. What you get with the Intel Itanium processor family are the characteristics built into the chip's architecture itself: the ability to handle tomorrow's problems from much bigger databases to rich media content and to do so in the most cost effective fashion. With the Intel Itanium platform, you can mine data and complete the analysis in a more timely and effective fashion, and with more reliability and availability of the system.

Today's jumbo-size databases and the need to handle incredibly higher levels of processing, networking, and security result from the IT revolution's own successes. Today, a CEO actually can demand and tap into huge amounts of information that have the ability to help manage his or her business. The Intel Itanium processor family, designed from the start with fully parallel instruction execution and a 64-bit address ability, is ideally suited to handle these needs.

About this Book

This book covers the development and application of the Intel Itanium processor family. It describes why the revolutionary leap forward in processing power can help CEOs achieve their company's vision. It also discusses the implication of these changes to a company's IT infrastructure. The final section of the book discusses the future of the Itanium architecture and the technological changes resulting from it. This will prove to be a helpful guide and forecaster.

---

1. Intel and Itanium are registered trademarks or trademarks of Intel Corporation or its subsidiaries in the United States and other countries.

Who Should Read This Book

This book is for CIOs, CEOs, IT managers, and technology managers. It has been written for the early adopters and those in the early majority who need to quickly and cost-effectively deploy Itanium-based solutions and transition their business to an Itanium-based infrastructure for increased performance and flexibility. While it is best to read through the entire work, the book is divided into four sections should you want to focus on a specific area of the Intel Itanium processor family.

Itanium Development

Chapters 1 through 4 are written specifically for CEOs, CIOs, CFOs, and C-level executives in general. The focus is on the development of the Itanium architecture at HP and Intel, why you should be aware of the coming Itanium revolution, and how it can help you develop your company's vision and attain goals of cost efficiency, productivity, and profits.

The opening chapters also introduce you to an idea that has been around for a long time in the technology world but can only now be pursued in a cost-effective manner: computing as a utility. We'll explore why computing is not just about hardware and software anymore. In the future, business will be moving to a model where you buy computing power as a *service,* not a *product.*

Architecture and Total Cost of Ownership

Chapters 5 through 9 narrow the theme to areas that a technology director will find of more direct concern. While continuing to discuss how the Intel Itanium platform is going to impact your business, we'll also spend time examining the true total cost of ownership. You'll see how you can get more processing power, more choices, and more flexibility for a lower overall cost, even in a mixed network environment.

In addition, the changes on the back end are discussed in detail. Where the Intel Itanium architecture is the next PA-RISC for Hewlett-Packard, to the average user the transition will be completely transparent. This is one of the implicit goals of the Intel Itanium platform, since the typical corporate knowledge worker should not have to struggle with what's behind the wall.

Transition Issues

In Chapters 10 through 16, we deal with the application of the Intel Itanium processor family. It directly addresses the issues of an IT manager or network engineer: when and how to get started in transitioning to the platform. A discussion of some early examples of the application of the Intel Itanium processor family architecture and the industry trends that drive the transition to it follows.

We also examine more technical issues, such as RISC versus CISC process-ing, how Explicitly Parallel Instruction Computing (EPIC) improves RISC, and how it can improve and simplify the needs of hardware, application software, and net-working. Of particular interest is adding reliability that is a major concern for server-centric systems and ways that Itanium-based systems correct soft errors that are built directly into the architecture.

These chapters also provide a transitional plan that follows these steps:

• Planning
• Informing
• Preparing
• Training

Future Itanium Development

Chapters 17 and 18 explore the next steps beyond the initial Intel Itanium plat-form rollout. In short, what does the future hold for the family's continued develop-ment and use in the corporate world? I'll share with you some of the anticipated development directions for this amazing chip family and the continued importance of compilers to the process.

Finally, we'll take a quick look at the rest of the value chain in the business of providing computer systems to you, including the chipsets and operating systems of the future and how they will be affected by the Intel Itanium architecture.

Towards the Intel Itanium Evolution

It's a truism in today's hype-laden world of technology that a lot of different items, be they hardware, software, or simply a new knowledge base, are labeled next gen-eration. However, you'll find after reading this book that the appellation in this case is justified. Why is that?

Because of the quantum leap that the Intel Itanium architecture makes in turn-ing high-end data processing into a cost-effective proposition, all of the other aspects of the IT revolution—networking, security, software development—will become easier, faster, and more reliable. The Intel Itanium architecture underpins all of these areas and gives them a solid boost.

So, pause a moment before rushing headlong into the use of the Intel Itanium processor family in a strictly corporate or IT department sense. It has been said that in order to know where you are going, it's helpful to see where you've been. On that note I invite you to take a moment to understand the history of the architecture's development and its growth as a major technical force of the future. Turn the page, and begin to understand why the Itanium processor family is so important and what it can really do for you.

Acknowledgements

Throughout the course of this work, there have been several people whose thoughts, ideas, and hard work have made a major impact on the final product. I'd like to acknowledge them as follows:

At Intel

Craig Barrett—Chief Executive Officer, Intel Corporation
Paul Otellini—President and Chief Operating Officer, Intel Corporation
Mike Graf—Product Line Manager, Itanium Processor Family
Bruce Morehead—Worldwide Applications Manager
John Kalvin—Field Sales Engineer
Lisa Hambrick—Intel Marketing Manager
John Crawford—Intel Fellow and Original Intel Architect on IPF

At Hewlett-Packard

Dirk Down—HP Marketing Communication Manger
Brian Cox—HP Product Marketing Manager
John Davis—HP Product Manager for HP-UX
Ken Kroeker—HP Systems Consulting
Gayle Malone—HP Consulting Services Manager
Jim Collins—HP Support Systems, Hardware
Tu-Ting Cheng—HP IPF Design Engineer
Sam Sudarsanam—HP Consulting Services

Katya Girgus—Marketing Consultant
Laura Lowell—Server Category Communications Manager
Brad Porter—Independent Consultant to HP on IPF Markets
John Santaferraro—Independent Consultant to HP on IPF Markets
Kurt Steele—Independent Consultant to HP on IPF Markets

Finally, I'd like to recognize the tireless work and dedication of those who have contributed directly to making this book a reality:

Pat Pekary—HP Books Publisher/Program Manager
Jill Harry—Executive Editor, Prentice Hall PTR
Kreg Wallace—Illustrator, Prentice Hall PTR
Val Fischer-Pallansch, Itanium Communications Manager
Michael Bellomo, MBA/JD—Special Manuscript Contributor

CHAPTER 1

Why Itanium Processors?
Benefits of the New
Processor Family

"The best, simplest way to describe the 'Mission Statement' for the Itanium family of microprocessors is: Creation of an architecture that can address future business needs with the best price-performance and flexibility."

—HP/Intel design team

In This Chapter:

- The Itanium architecture 'Mission Statement'
- The Itanium Processor Family
- Benefits of Itanium processors for different platforms
- Handling Legacy Software, Hardware, and Data
- Reasons for Itanium Processor Performance Value
- Itanium Processor Family in the Enterprise Environment

In this day and age, most of us are familiar with the Silicon-valley buzzword, the 'killer app'—the creation of a software application that can do so much more than its predecessors that it's bound to create tremendous demand. However, it's less often that you hear about a 'killer chip' that will enhance information technology infrastructure to the degree that it is nothing short of a revolution. Yet that is exactly what the Intel® Itanium® processor family[1] architecture is capable of—by building

1.   Intel and Itanium are registered trademarks of Intel Corporations or its subsidiaries in the United States and other countries.

1

on, and then breaking away from established computing principles so that it becomes the industry's new application performance leader.

What you're seeing with Itanium development is the result of heavy investments by both Intel and Hewlett-Packard in a brand new microprocessor family. Yet this is not a matter of breaking with their established system and environments. It's an evolution, not a revolution—one that provides for maximum transition and flexibility—adding value with minimal risk to customers.

Itanium Mission Statement

The Itanium processor family came about for several reasons, but the primary one was that the processor architecture advances of RISC were no longer growing at the rate seen in the 1980's or the 1990's. Yet, customers continued to demand greater application performance, due to the following developments:

• Increased users and demand (internet)
• Higher bandwidth tasks (streaming)
• Requirements for secure processing (SSL)
• Larger hardware requirements (Very Large Data Bases)
• Support for multi-OS environments (virtual data center, computing as a utility)

The Itanium processor family was developed as a response to address the future performance and growth needs of business, technical, and scientific users with greater flexibility, better performance, and a much greater 'bang for the buck' in the price-performance arena.

The Itanium Processor Family

The Itanium architecture was designed to be the new industry standard in high performance processor architecture for the next twenty years. The Itanium processor captures the best-in-class application performance for technical and enterprise computing out of the box today. However, given the continued development of chips and compilers for this unique architecture, its long-term future is also bright.

The Itanium processor starts out with a strong price/performance ratio and is designed to take advantage of scalability gains. This is assisted by broad industry support led by both HP and Intel, who created the initial microprocessor architecture from an alliance of their best R&D resources. This new instruction set architecture, based on HP/Intel co-developer knowledge, has enabled the creation of a strong microprocessor 'roadmap' as indicated in Figure 1-1.

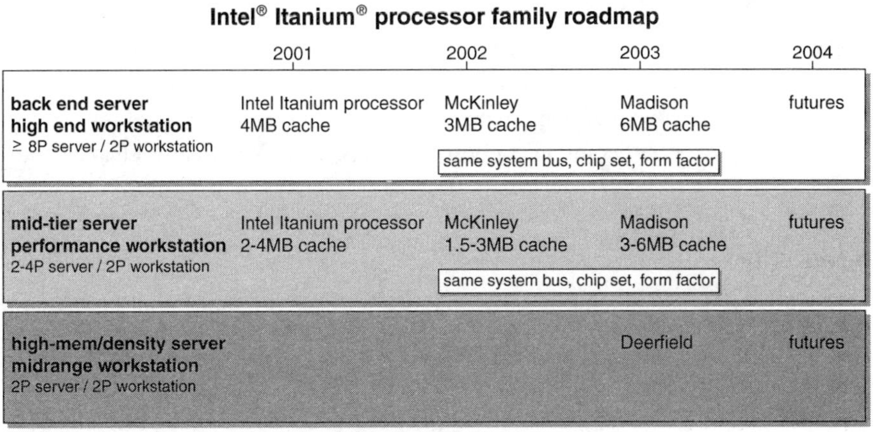

Intel® Itanium® processor family roadmap

	2001	2002	2003	2004
back end server **high end workstation** ≥ 8P server / 2P workstation	Intel Itanium processor 4MB cache	McKinley 3MB cache	Madison 6MB cache	futures
		same system bus, chip set, form factor		
mid-tier server **performance workstation** 2-4P server / 2P workstation	Intel Itanium processor 2-4MB cache	McKinley 1.5-3MB cache	Madison 3-6MB cache	futures
		same system bus, chip set, form factor		
high-mem/density server **midrange workstation** 2P server / 2P workstation			Deerfield	futures

Figure 1-1 The Itanium Processor Family Roadmap

How Will I Benefit if I Run a RISC-Based System?

Enterprises that run RISC-based systems gain an immediate benefit from the switch to an Itanium®-based platform. The lower hardware costs and multi-vendor OS strengths of the new industry-standard architecture, Explicitly Parallel Instruction Computing (EPIC), provide for the following benefits:

- Multi-OS support
- Lower overall Cost of Ownership for enterprise IT
- Assurance of leading performance and scalability over the long-term

How Will I Benefit if I Run an IA-32 Based System?

IA-32 based system users will see immediate performance gains when taking on more complex workloads and processing large amounts of data. Areas that are less sensitive to performance can transition to the new architecture on an as-needed basis. Organizations that move to an Itanium-based platform can address current performance issues points today and gain familiarity with architecture that will be able to keep up with scalable demands in the near and intermediate future. These demands include:

- Greater memory addressability
- More complex applications and computing environments
- Secure web server transactions
- Computer aided design such as Mechanical Analysis
- Very large memory databases
- Industry-standard servers in every tier of the data center

Itanium RAS Features

The information technology industry's term RAS is one that applies directly to Itanium. 'RAS,' or 'Reliability—Availability—Serviceability' provides an excellent example of the benefits that Itanium brings to clients. In each case, Itanium can provide a benefit that is either unique or best in its class compared to less advanced processors.

Reliability

'Reliability' refers to the ability of the hardware to avoid failing. With the Itanium processor family, this ability is built directly into the processor. The prime example of the improved reliability of the processor is the built-in 'error correcting memory.' In a large system with megabytes of cache memory, a little thing like an alpha particle coming through the atmosphere can hit one of the memory circuits and change one of the bits. A change in the bit means that the value in the memory has also been altered.

An alpha particle strike is an example of a purely random error that occurs from environmental causes even though no "hard" failure has happened. It's not the result of a bad design or a component failure. However, the error correcting memory will fix the problem on the fly guarding against this effect.

This is because error correction introduces of 'parity check' that can tell whether a given bit should be 'on' or 'off', and even fix the piece of data.

Availability

A system with 100% 'Availability' is a system that is always up and never down. At present, the 100% threshold is only theoretically attainable, in part due to the unpredictability of random errors, natural disasters, required maintenance, upgrades and of course 'hard' and 'soft' errors. Typically, the reason systems tend to crash and go down is due to these last two kinds of errors.

Hard Errors and Soft Errors

A 'hard' error, as the name implies, is where something is physically changed on the system, or a piece of hardware crashes, freezes, or burns up. This can happen to a power supply if it shorts out, a coolant fan that seizes up, or a component that short-circuits. Hard errors also include outside interference that results in downtime—such as a lightning strike that causes a power surge, resulting in knocked out equipment.

A 'soft error' is of the type described in the previous section on reliability. Here a cosmic ray or electrical noise on a bus will unintentionally and randomly reset a data bit. But the parity and error correcting code circuits (ECC) of the Itanium processor will actually fix these errors as they are detected and keep the user's computing environment safe in spite of these unexpected events. The on-chip parity checks and ecc will detect and correct both hard and soft errors.

Software Errors

Software Errors, as the name implies, are errors that occur in the software. They typically occur when software has encountered something in the programming or data that confuses the program or is unanticipated by the programmer, so the program doesn't know where it is going, or what it should do next.

Sometimes these errors could be initially caused by faulty hardware (a hard error leading to a software error) or by programming mistakes. For example, this could be caused by a situation where a program is trying to branch to an address in memory and that address happens to be in the middle of a block of data or in open memory.

Ideally, the system should be able to catch these software errors without having to stop and wait for some kind of operator or other intervention. The best result is that the system has a place to go and 'recover' from the error and not crash. An example would be allowing the program to jump to a new address. This allows it to back up and take a look at what happened to keep executing at a slower speed, or even go into the execution process to generate a recovery in a graceful way. It may even go into another routine that 'branches' around the area with the problem.

Serviceability

Let's say that as a network administrator you find out that nothing is being received over a specific network node. Investigating, you find an I/O card has gone out on the system. On a typical Itanium-based system, you can pull out the card while the system is still running and plug another one in—it's 'instantly serviceable.' You don't have to shut the machine off.

Hewlett-Packard computers typically have system component redundancies for subsystems like fans, and power supplies. We tend to build the redundancy into the areas that statistically tend to have the most failures. Thus if the fan fails, the entire unit doesn't burn up. Similarly, built into the architecture is the enabling capability to allow for OLR (Online Replacement). This is another way of saying that you can pull out a component (e.g., I/O card) while a system is running, and keep on going. Instead of engaging in costly downtime, replacement can be done on the fly.

This is a capability that has been built into the architecture. In a multi-processor situation, you can turn off one processor and substitute in a new one. The ability to service the machine while it is still running reduces your down time even further. It's rather like being able to replace a flat on your car while in the middle of your freeway commute.

Reasons for Itanium®-based Platform Value

The Itanium architecture achieves a more difficult goal than a processor that could have been designed with 'price as no object'. Rather, it delivers near-peerless speed at a price that is sustainable by the mainstream corporate market. Some of the features that this processor brings to the table follow below. Other reasons, such as the parallel architecture, are important enough to discuss in their own separate sections in this chapter, which follow.

- Floating-point performance for compute intensive applications
- EPIC technology for maximum parallelism & HW/SW synergy
- Scalability from 1-way to 128-way+
- 64-bit addressing and high bandwidth

Highly Parallel Architecture

The highly parallel architecture of the Itanium architecture allows the processor to get more things done during each 'clock cycle'. There are typically two ways to speed up the performance of a processor. The one that the general public understands and follows is to increase the 'clock speed' of a processor. For years, this has been the initial benchmark as to how to measure the speed of a chip—a 500Mhz Pentium versus a 200Mhz Cyrix chip, for example.

Members of the Itanium processor family will have a clock speed of one gigahertz and greater. Of course, we're all excited about being able to hasten the clock speed to such a degree. Increasing the clock rate will improve performance, but the processor is still bound by the architecture that defines its operation. For example, the processor may be an early implementation of RISC, which will attempt to get only a single instruction completed per cycle.

Imagine the performance gain from completing two instructions per clock cycle instead of one. By doing two things in parallel, it's the equivalent of doubling the clock speed on the microprocessor. Consider that if you had a 500Mhz chip that could process two instructions per clock cycle, you would end up with a one-gigahertz microprocessor without the costs associated with the higher clock rate.

This ability to make these leaps of performance was the reason we made the step in RISC to move to what's called 'superscalar out-of-order execution RISC'. The end goal was specifically to be able to do more things in parallel, and create a speed gain where previously, the main method was to keep increasing clock speed and changing the manufacturing process to "shrink" the chip

HP and Intel created EPIC—an explicitly parallel instruction computing architecture, which is the heart of why the Itanium processor family can create its unique price-performance signature. This allows us to go from a slightly more than one instruction per cycle to up to 6 instructions per cycle with the current generation of processors. This level of parallelism is probably not likely over an entire application, but by getting a boost in even a couple of critical loops, the overall effect on the speed of processing can be significant.

In performance tests in the lab, we've seen 1 gigahertz Itanium processors running alongside 2.6-gigahertz chips, and the Itanium processors are getting more usable application work done—because of the unique architecture.

The magic of EPIC is in its parallelism. Of course, it does take some work in the compiler, and it does take some sorting out to queue up the information to the microprocessor; you have to know that you can do certain things in parallel. And the future of this technology is just beginning. As compilers get better, and we continue our research into the methods of properly utilizing parallel architecture, we'll be able to get even more speed and performance gains out of this processor family.

Investment Protection

The triple protection that Itanium architecture offers is for legacy software, legacy hardware, and legacy data. This was the second major goal we had when we began the project. We wanted to protect the customer's investment in IT infrastructure as much as possible.

Legacy Software

It turns out that when you analyze an organization's IT investment, the bulk of it is not in the hardware. Most of the investment beyond the people is in the software and the legacy data that is stored. So one of the goals when developing Itanium was being able to run—even though it would be at a lower speed than a native binary—the existing applications coming from both the IA-32 world as well as the PA-RISC world.

HP built this investment protection for PA-RISC into HP-UX, our version of the UNIX®2 operating system. For the IA-32 world, the backward compatibility is also implemented, allowing even more flexibility. This allows Itanium-based systems to run Linux applications and Microsoft Windows applications without change.

The idea is that the user won't have to immediately go out and update new software applications. Most customers will want to update some applications in order to take full advantage of the phenomenal speed gains the Itanium processor family makes available, but in some cases, it's just not a critical issue. For example, the application in question could be a utility routine that runs in the background, say to monitor events and generate reports. An example would be HP's Openview suite of system management tools. In other words, it would be a program that would stand

---

2.   UNIX is a registered trademark of The Open Group.

to benefit extremely little from an performance upgrade, and yet would be annoying or laborious to re-compile or re-write.

A second problem that IT organizations often run into is in their own proprietary software. This is where the source code has been lost and the person who wrote it is no longer available to consult. The cause of this loss is irrelevant. What matters is that there is no one around to redesign the program on short notice. With the investment protection, built into Itanium-based systems so that a redesign isn't necessary, this issue is neatly avoided.

Legacy Hardware

Hewlett-Packard's long-standing policy on legacy hardware was extended to the Itanium architecture before the project even began in earnest. The goal here was to build systems that we could upgrade from PA-RISC microprocessors by simply replacing the systems board with future Itanium processors installed. So most of the Hewlett Packard PA-RISC systems that we've built and launched in the past year have the ability to be upgraded to versions of the Itanium processor family.

Legacy Data

Enterprises have huge databases built over time on their IT systems. This data, if built under a PA-RISC and HP-UX environment, is stored in a "big endian" format. If you move to a system, which is "little endian", the user can't simply plug the older disk with its data into the new system. (See Appendix A for a definition of "endian.") Instead, the data will need to be converted before being used. In order to protect the data of our enterprise customers on HP-UX systems, as well as data that is stored in "little endian" on Windows or Linux based systems, we made sure that Itanium was endian neutral and could handle data in either format.

Choice and Breadth of Operating Systems and Applications

A real frustration for customers is when the application needed is not available under the operating system that is currently installed and running on a system. For example, you may be running Microsoft Windows, but the application you want runs only under Unix. Often, you're left with only one option—going back to the application vendor and asking them if they can develop a version of the application that will work under your installed operating system.

Many IT organizations today are concerned with the mix of computers using different operating systems on a single network. This has been caused in part by the gradual dominance of the front-end applications by Windows, while the back end continues to use UNIX or other non-Microsoft systems. There's a legitimate concern that a major investment in one type of operating system will result in a severe disadvantage should the investment prove to be in the 'wrong' one.

Under the Itanium processor family, a maximum amount of choice is preserved. You can continue running UNIX or OpenVMS on the back end, for instance, but if the world switched over to Windows or Linux the following day, the impact is minimized. Of course, you'd have to get new applications, but instead of having to replace your hardware you could phase in a transition without the major capital expense and hassle involved in complete replacement.

Enterprise Technology

The basic definition of 'enterprise computing' is the type of computing that is done in large companies on high-bandwidth networks, as opposed to 'personal' computing, which tends to take place on stand-alone machines. Most enterprise computing is done in large corporations, so the emphasis is on which systems work best with business-to-business (B2B) applications. These B2B applications include programs written for supply chain management, customer relationship management, communications/sales tracking, and project/milestone management.

This form of computing can also be determined by the following characteristics:

- Large databases with the need to update, analyze, and mine the data constantly.
- The need for reliability/available/scalability 24 by 7.
- Large applications.
- Hundreds or thousands of users.
These requirements are also expressed graphically, as in Figure 1-2.

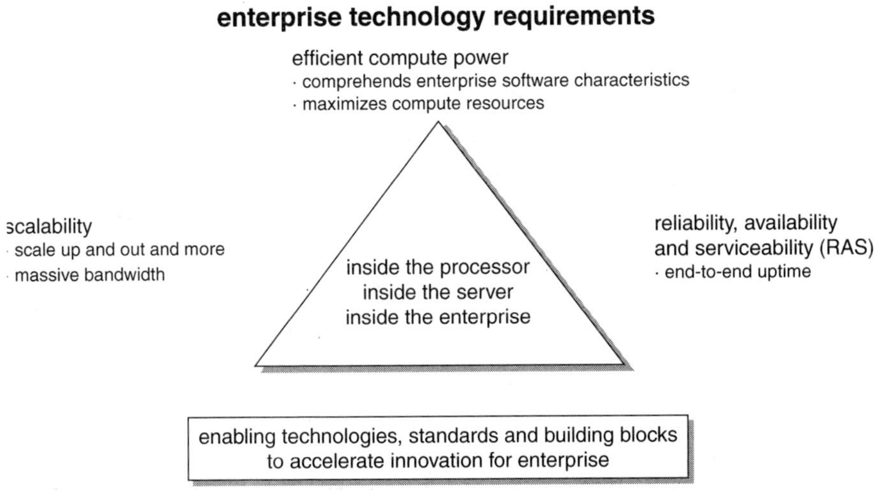

enterprise technology requirements

efficient compute power
· comprehends enterprise software characteristics
· maximizes compute resources

scalability
· scale up and out and more
· massive bandwidth

inside the processor
inside the server
inside the enterprise

reliability, availability
and serviceability (RAS)
· end-to-end uptime

enabling technologies, standards and building blocks
to accelerate innovation for enterprise

Figure 1-2   Diagram of Enterprise Technology Requirements

How Itanium Architecture Affects Enterprise Computing

The Intel Itanium architecture was intended to extend further into the enterprise by improving upon capabilities of today's architectures. Enterprise IT environments are extremely heterogeneous, with multiple system, applications, and operating systems. An example of this can be found at Hewlett-Packard itself. It's not uncommon to find UNIX servers, which need to talk to a Windows or Linux servers, which in turn service PCs that are running the latest version of Microsoft Windows.

A multiple, heterogeneous environment is much more the norm today than one which is dedicated exclusively to a single operating system or set of enterprise applications. Itanium's ability to handle just about any operating system that is run on it makes it a natural fit for today's mixed network environments

In Summary

- The Itanium architecture was developed to meet and exceed future performance and growth needs of enterprise business, technical, and scientific users with greater flexibility and future headroom. The idea was to create an architecture capable of greater speed and also unbeatable price-performance.

- The Intel Itanium processor is faster than most of the present day competition. And, with future compiler improvements and newer chip designs, it will outpace all other existing architectures.

- No matter if you run RISC or IA-32 based systems, you'll still be able to reap performance gains from Itanium-based systems.

- An Itanium-based platform also provides superior performance in all three areas of 'RAS': 'Reliability—Availability—Serviceability'.

- The Itanium processor uses EPIC, or explicitly parallels instruction computing architecture. This allows a system to go from one instruction per cycle to 6 or even more instructions per cycle.

- Investment protection was another goal of Itanium-based solutions. The triple protection that Itanium-based systems offer is for legacy software, legacy hardware, and legacy data. This is due in part to Itanium's ability to work with almost any operating system and application.

- Enterprise computing is an ideal place for Itanium power. By improving upon capabilities of today's architectures, Itanium can ensure flexibility and choice in the enterprise environment.

The Itanium Processor Family: The Next Generation of Processor Architecture

"There's not a single advantage to Itanium. There's a set of advantages that lead you to want to use it. Business advantages, technology advantages...it's a 64-bit architecture and that's going to be very important to the positioning of [an Itanium-based system] as a high-end server platform. And then...you give somebody 64 gigabytes or more of memory, they'll use it."

—Jerry Huck, Lead HP Architect on the Itanium Project

In this Chapter:

- The Need for Itanium Power
- Development of Early Architectures
- PA-RISC
- Beyond Megahertz = Speed
- Moore's Second Law and how Itanium Suspends It

Jerry Huck, one of Hewlett-Packard's designers behind the creation of the Intel® Itanium® Processor family,[3] holds the opinion that the development of the chip's architecture embodies the third great wave of innovation in the field of microprocessor design. Far from being alone in this opinion, he's actually in very good

---

3.   Intel, Itanium, and Pentium are registered trademarks or trademarks of Intel Corporation or its subsidiaries in the United States and other countries.

company with several of the leading lights in his area of expertise. John Crawford, an Intel Fellow, shared the platform with him at the October 1997 Microprocessor Forum and described the coming chip as one that could crunch data in 64-bit chunks at a time, as opposed to 32 for the then dominant Intel® Pentium® processor.

It would be tempting to mistake the coming Intel Itanium architecture—and its the entire family of processors slated for release in the coming months—as yet another high-end processor. Yet the development of the Itanium processor is more than a simple line extension. As a product, the Itanium processor is the chip platform that will enable HP and Intel to stand out as a technology pioneers in an industry that is rapidly falling victim to mass commoditization. The reasons have to do with the explosive growth and demands placed on servers in the information technology arena, the evolving need for more efficient processor architecture, and a profound shift in the way computing is being viewed in both the academic and corporate arena.

Technology Shifts and the Need For Itanium Processor Power

From a hardware point of view, the "high growth" market for Intel architecture machines has shifted from personal computers to network servers. This can be accomplished, if not in the most efficient manner, by having the machine "tricked out" with extra memory and a load of extra disk drives. However, the growth of the Internet has led to an exponential increase in the demands placed on these kinds of servers.

No matter how extensive the upgrades, the personal computing processors— top of the line Pentiums and their clone offshoots—are simply not enough. The microprocessor 'engines' that were originally designed to drive workstations remain too unscalable to effectively handle today's server demands. More recently, the prevailing shift has been towards machines specifically designed to handle the extra load.

The Rise of the Network Server

Today's corporate computing departments have effectively migrated from the "big iron" surrounded by PCs model to clients-connected to a peer-to-peer network of servers spanning multiple enterprises. Specifically, the move has been toward UNIX®4-based servers made by companies such as Sun Microsystems, IBM (yes, even the mainframe giant), and of course, Hewlett-Packard—especially the new HP which also now includes Compaq. This decision to place more computing power at network nodes is based on two main factors.

4.   UNIX is a registered trademark of The Open Group.

First, the 'heavy lifting' enterprise and scientific and engineering computing tasks are ones that need reliability and high availability as well as speed. The use of UNIX as the operating system of choice to run for example, sensitive financial, scientific, modeling, or data warehousing applications is directly related to how valuable the data involved has become. This market is important to the degree that each of the main vendors of Unix based systems have their own 'flavor' of the Unix operating system: Sun Microsystems runs Solaris, IBM uses AIX, and HP runs HP-UX.

Second, the companies and organizations that have the need for such heavy computing power have not extensively used PC-based servers for a very simple fact. Most PC-based chip families lack the reliability and basic horsepower needed to drive complex, compute resource-intensive applications. UNIX servers typically incorporate more powerful microprocessors to begin with, and this trend continues and is accelerated by the implementation of Itanium®-based servers.

Itanium-based Systems Ideal for the Network Server

The Intel Itanium processor family is well positioned to take advantage of these ongoing customer needs. For example, systems powered by Itanium processors can handle the large datasets and bandwidth-intensive applications that are utilized by major corporations. Also, Itanium based systems can easily integrate and manage large databases that are typical of applications built on software from Oracle®5 and Microsoft®6 as well as IBM (Informix and DB2).

Companies that need a large amount of fast, powerful computing power also stand to benefit from the Itanium architecture's rollout. If a major capital investment has been made in earlier versions of either Microsoft, Linux,®7 or HP-UX software, complete backward compatibility is successfully retained. In addition, needs such as complex modeling and design, or projects that require maximum scalability, headroom for the future, and investment protection will realize major benefits from the Itanium architecture. Because it is based on an industry standard architecture backed by volume manufacturing, Itanium-based systems can decisively claim the ability to run a computing environment at a significantly lower cost than a comparable RISC-based system.

Development of Early Architectures

The instruction set architecture (ISA) that drives the chip design goes hand in hand with the complexity and power of the microprocessor itself. For example, the early x86 architecture was explicitly made to work with the cutting-edge technology of

---

5.   Oracle is a registered U.S. trademark of Oracle Corporation, Redwood City, California.
6.   Microsoft is a U.S. registered trademark of Microsoft Corp.
7.   Linux is a registered trademark of Linus Torvalds.

the time: a processor that contained transistors that numbered in the tens of thousands. Later instruction sets, such as RISC, were designed to work with processors that contained hundreds of thousands up to millions of transistors.

By contrast, the next generation of processors will make an additional jump and contain transistors numbering in the 10's and 100's of millions. Preliminary estimates of the current family of processors put the transistor count above the range of twenty million. These incredibly high transistor counts come from the advances in IC process technology, which is at 0.18 microns today, and will continue to shrink in future designs.

CISC—State of the Art in the 60's and 70's

CISC stands for Complex Instruction Set Computing, a style of instruction-set architecture that is best exemplified by the x86 or IA-32 ISA. While CISC dates back to the 1960's, it really only began to impact the computing world in a big way in the late 1970's. In 1978, the first processor to feature the x86 ISA, the 8086, was mass-produced. While cutting edge for its time, this processor suffered from many design limitations.

This included the small register files, which consisted of sixteen 8-bit registers, with several devoted to special uses. In addition, there were similar limitations with the floating-point (FP) register file, and awkward segment addressing.

RISC—Simpler Computing in the 80's

It has been said that as CISC developed, the computer scientists, designers, and developers continued to develop with CISC-based architecture due to concurrent advances in technology. For example, the price and density of memory technology (RAM) began to fall dramatically. The development of 'dynamic RAM', which 'loses' its memory unless it is refreshed with electrical current, further reduced the hardware cost of supporting CISC. These advances allowed CISC to be expanded, instead of discontinued, in favor of a simpler, more efficient architecture.

RISC, or Reduced Instruction Set Computing, refers to microprocessor chips that implement fewer instructions than CISC chips with the goal of executing one or more instructions per clock cycle. The complex instructions from a CISC implementation are constructed by using several of the simpler RISC instructions to perform the same task. First introduced in the early 1980's, RISC was a reaction to the limitations imposed by the inherent design of CISC by researchers at IBM, Stanford, and the University of California at Berkeley. Logically, the main driving force behind the development and promulgation of RISC was to make a more efficient CPU by having fewer, simpler instructions that could be executed faster. The key ideas have been summarized in a 1979 report as follows:

- Increasing the register set size from eight to 32 registers.
- Creating fix-length instructions, typically 32 bits wide.
- Simpler instruction coding.
- Load/store architecture.
- No self-modifying code.

Because of the performance gain derived from RISC, it quickly became the de facto standard for higher end computers. RISC eventually ran into its own set of limitations, which in turn led to the Itanium architecture development.

Architecture Families at Hewlett-Packard

Through the 70's and into the next decade, HP had ended up supporting three separate architectures. Each form had been commercially successful to one degree or another and had proprietary OS's (Operating Systems), I/O devices, network components, and compilers. It was a challenge for HP to continue supporting a family of diverse architectures. To a great degree, HP was suffering from its own design excellence—customers wanted to continue using architectures that were ten or more years old, which could still meet their business demands. HP was supporting each of the following:

- HP-3000: A 16-bit architecture, which was an early, distributed commercial transaction processing system.
- HP-1000: The then current leader in process control and data acquisition systems.
- HP-9000: Based originally on the Motorola 68000 series, this architecture was primarily used on series of workstations and controllers.

By 1981, the logistics of balancing all three architecture families was becoming more challenging. This challenge was given to Hewlett-Packard's central research organization, the HP Labs, to consolidate the three separate architectures into a single workable system.

The results were successful, as it led to the subsequent development of the new technology, called PA-RISC. This new form of architecture proved to be scalable and gave HP leadership in the performance arena. Just as critically, it proved to be a leader in the price/performance ratio across an extremely broad range of applications.

The Development of PA-RISC

PA-RISC proved to be a boon for Hewlett-Packard through the rest of the 80's and into the 90's, as it coincided with the trend to open client/server computing. The reliance of this sort of computing on the UNIX operating system allowed HP to establish its own brand, HP-UX, as a major player in the UNIX world.

Former CEO Lew Platt noted that there would be several opportunities to enhance PA-RISC, but that at some point it would 'run out of steam' and HP would need a next generation architecture. To that end, a team was created to work on this very possibility. Platt notes that the team was made up of people "whom we had acquired from some organizations that were working on very advanced computing techniques. So we brought in some really world class experts who...began work on the next generation architecture."

Joel Birnbaum, HP's Chief Technical Officer and General Manager of the HP labs at the time, noted in his presentation at the Microprocessor Forum in 1997 that the designers in the lab were able to extend the life of the PA-RISC architecture by adding several new innovations, such as out-of-order execution. Concern over the increasing level of design complexity began to grow again. This was because excessive complexity could prove limiting due to the now large base of installed PA-RISC systems. The solution found was known internally at Hewlett-Packard as 'wide word,' and that turned out to influence the next architectural differentiation at the system-wide level in the following decade.

CEO Platt remembers that at the start, 'wide word'—which would eventually evolve into the Itanium architecture—was one that was thought of as too far ahead of the curve initially. Yet he mentions, in an instance of foresight, that "if you're going to make a mistake, probably a good one to make is to be there with a new architecture ahead of when you need it, instead of after."

As the project began to develop beyond its initial stages it became obvious that the project's special architecture had tremendous potential. Beyond the synergy that resulted from the partnership with Intel, Platt noted that it would "represent a large step forward from where we were with PA-RISC at that point in time, and it really had a very long future ahead of it."

Beyond Speed and onto Capabilities

Paul Otellini, Intel's Chief Operations Officer, probably said it best when he spoke about the changing dynamic that drives the need for Itanium and its processor family. "With Itanium the definition somewhat changes because it's not about megahertz anymore, it's about all of the functionality together."

The standard speed benchmark, touted by computer stores and resellers alike, has been speed as measured in 'megahertz'. And it is true that for most architectures in the last two decades, the megahertz measurement has been a good representative of relative performance. On the other hand, a company's IT managers might have a slightly different evaluation process. Paul notes that "they run benchmarks, they run the real applications against it and in those environments, megahertz is not the only, nor the best surrogate for performance. How you deal with processing in a mega-hertz [is only part of] the equation."

This goes to the heart of how Itanium is changing the way computing will be viewed in the coming years. For example, Paul noted that one of the largest institutions on Wall Street was about to convert their entire trading back end to one that is totally Itanium-based.

"What they will see is an increase in performance by a factor of ten, which to a firm such as this one equals a tremendous benefit in terms of cost efficiency and cost savings. The emphasis again is not on how powerful the machine is that sits on their desk, or the operating system that is the primary user interface. Instead, what really counts is the speed and flexibility of the overall application."

In a way, this allows Itanium architecture to again be the right product implemented at the right time. As Joel Birnbaum had said, we had always felt there was "...an insatiable need for more performance—bigger, better, faster...Now we didn't know that the Internet would have such a major impact, we didn't know that every time you logged into your system there would be all these windows and communication with 40 different servers to even say hello." Yet it is this increased performance requirement, particularly over a heavily trafficked network, which creates the need for Itanium-based systems.

Moore's First Law and Its Impact

Moore's Law is the prediction made by one of Intel's founders, Gordon Moore, that the number of transistors that engineers could place onto a microchip would double every 18 months. This in turn meant that CPU power would increase accordingly every year and a half. The graphic representation of this can be seen in Figure 2-1 below. This was a benefit to the computer scientist and other power hungry commercial users who always needed faster equipment. Also, this became a shorthand way for computer systems vendors to predict that they would be able to double performance every 18 months.

To date, Moore's first law has remained unchanged, as technological advances have continued to confound those who predicted the demise of its overly optimistic assumptions. Where the limitation was going to be the optics to align the silicon wafers, a solution was found to work around it. Another time, the light waves themselves used were supposed to be too coarse to make even smaller electronic lines—but clever engineers solved this issue by switching to UV light, which has an even shorter wavelength than the visible light spectrum normally used.

This in turn set up a separate phenomenon in the computer software industry that paralleled the continued rise in processing power. As processors can handle more and more data and task instructions, applications have quickly moved to seize upon the greater amount of power on any given computer.

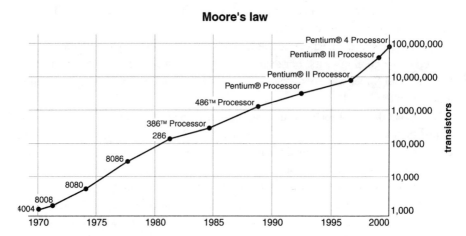

Figure 2-1 Graphic Representation of Moore's Law

This has had a real impact on enterprise applications. Many applications today such as Oracle Financial products or Enterprise Resource Planning (ERP) solutions from SAP simply cannot run efficiently except on the latest machines. When users want to run the latest application's bells and whistles but find that their performance is restricted, they will naturally turn to a faster machine.

Moore's Second Law and How the Itanium Architecture Suspends It

In 1994, Moore postulated a second law that qualified his first one. Interestingly enough, the law he cited was not so much technological in nature as economic. Although increasingly sophisticated tools can be used to cram ever more transistors onto a chip, the price of the manufacturing expertise rises accordingly.

Over the past three decades, the cost of a chip fabrication plant has soared so high as to make percentage comparisons meaningless. The plant is easily the most expensive facility that the industry has to purchase, especially taking environmental costs into consideration. In 1966, a plant might have cost $14 million, whereas a plant with similar output today has a sticker-shock price tag of one and a half *billion* dollars or more. This can be seen in Figure 2-2.

Therefore, the cost of increasing the number of transistors that can be put on the chip cannot help but increase even as the size of the circuits on the chip shrinks. Even though chip-making giants like Intel will be able to afford the more expensive and precise plants, the cost to the end users of the systems may increase faster than the increase in performance supplied by the new designs. The 'slack' in the equation so far is in the ability of the fabrication plants to make gains in both chip density,

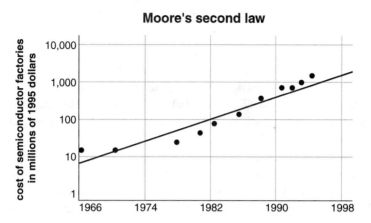

Figure 2-2   Graphic Representation of Moore's Second Law

and in wafer output. At HP, we were seeing a slightly different effect of Moore's Second law.

With our RISC designs, typically, placing more transistors onto a chip did increase its abilities, but as we tried to add more capabilities to existing RISC designs, an incrementally greater percentage of the transistors became tied up in overhead to manage the added complexity of RISC. Design improvements such as out-of-order execution, which was very helpful in speeding up complex ERP applications, increased the overhead faster than the added performance. The billion-dollar fabrication plant may be placing a record number of transistors on the CPU chip. However, the net cost of the chips was increasing faster than the gain in power from the new designs.

This is where the Itanium processor arrives and suspends Moore's Second law. The Itanium processor family's unique architecture allows the processor to break away from the higher and higher percentages soaked up in overhead, allowing a performance gain that is unlike anything else in the market. Rather than spending to gain a top-notch fabrication plant for producing chips with moderate speed gains, the Itanium microprocessor takes advantage of both the speed gains from the manufacturing process and the next generation architecture to give superior performance for a much more attractive price.

It's this promise of lower price for superior processing power that will allow companies and research organizations to continue pursuing the trends of today's IT market. Higher levels of electronic commerce, handling streaming video, data mining, and complex problem solving that were once unheard of except on supercomputers will become possible in a much shorter period of time. The idea of computing as a service or as a utility becomes a reality, as computing can now be both more efficient and cost effective at the same time. We'll explore more of this emerging model in the next chapter.

In Summary

- The microprocessor 'engines' that run computers at present have inherent limits on parallelism, scalability, and reliability to effectively handle newer, more complex computing challenges. The emerging need is for newer machines that can handle the extra demands placed on servers today.
- Enterprises that need large amount of analytical, "number crunching" computing power will gain immediate benefits from the Intel Itanium architecture. This is because systems powered by an Itanium processor have improved floating-point mathematical power and can handle larger datasets and bandwidth-hungry applications.
- The early architectures such as CISC and RISC paved the way for the Itanium architecture development. The synergy resulting from the partnership with Intel enabled Itanium technology to leapfrog forward beyond RISC technologies to create the next 20-year architecture.
- Moore's First Law results in the spiraling increase in microprocessor power. This has resulted in a parallel phenomenon in the computer software industry: That is, as microprocessors and systems can handle more data and process it faster, applications grow to use the greater amount of power available on any given computer.
- Moore's Second Law, which addresses the rapidly increasing cost of producing faster and more advanced chips by shrinking the line size and requiring new plants and equipment, is mitigated by the Itanium architecture. This is because Itanium's advantage comes from more efficient use of the transistors on the chip by eliminating the overhead created by high performance out-of-order execution RISC designs. Instead, the transistors on the chip are used to directly increase the power and to provide a "multiplier" to the clock speed, allowing a large price-performance gain.

Planning the Revolution: Developing the Itanium Processor Family

"Wherever you see a high density of intellectual property and a high density of human capital going into the design of a product, you can in fact accelerate this [process] with computing power...You can expand the creativity of your employees...and translate those ideas into marketable designs or marketable products much more rapidly."

—Craig Barrett, President of Intel

In This Chapter:

- Itanium Architecture's Dual Legacy
- The Developments in Computing Power Leading to the Itanium Processor Family.
- The Wide Word Project's Charter
- The Findings of Itanium's Design Team
- The Reasons Behind a Partnership with Intel
- Envisioning a World with Itanium Computing Power

The Itanium Processor Family: Built on Two Impressive Legacies

At the heart of this next wave in computing power is the next generation of computing architectures, the Intel® Itanium® processor family. This was the result of a joint development project between Hewlett-Packard and Intel®[8] Corporation. Intel, with

---

8.   Intel, Itanium, and Pentium are registered trademarks or trademarks of Intel Corporation in the
      United States and other countries.

its four-fifths share of the PC microprocessor market and proven ability in microprocessor design and volume production, was a key partner in the project. Hewlett-
Packard, also one of the top five producers of microprocessors, came with a slightly
different skill set. HP's direction was from the more high value workstation- and
server-centric side.

In fact, HP's approach brought unique strengths to this project. There was
already a synergy to build on—the PA-RISC architecture and Hewlett-Packard's
own flavor of UNIX, HP-UX. PA-RISC was the first form of the RISC architecture that was widely available commercially. PA-RISC, with its simpler instruction set that allowed one or more complete instructions to be executed on a single
clock cycle, exhibited a significant performance gain over existing architectures at
the time.

HP-UX was the first flavor of UNIX to feature significant commercial application support. HP-UX, particularly HP-UX 11i, perfectly complements the use of
the PA-RISC architecture by providing stability and scalability—allowing PA-RISC
to work to its maximum capability in the enterprise environment.

Several forces contributed to and enhanced the creation of the Intel Itanium
architecture. The reasons for its development stemmed from more than a reaction to
the market forces driving the need for more sophisticated forms of computing. At
work was the highly successful long-term strategy that HP formulated in the 1990's.

You'll learn about how Hewlett-Packard, together with Intel, determined
which direction the next generation of architecture was going to take. You'll also see
why this collaboration has yielded the next generation of processor architecture,
driven by the collective abilities of the best minds in the field. And finally, you'll
start to see how it will move enterprises and partners into the forefront of this technological revolution.

The Progress of Technology at Hewlett-Packard

As hard as it is to imagine today in the world of technology companies, dot-com
blowouts and single product plays, Hewlett-Packard's first computer was introduced
almost four decades ago. From this early generation of machines—the 'Instrument
Automator' and the general-purpose "alpha"—the basic groundwork had been laid
to develop the fledging operating system and system software, all of which had to
run on a 16-bit-per-word, 8 kilobyte system.

The hardware for the "alpha" project became known commercially as the HP
3000, which targeted the general-purpose business market in the early 1970's. The
demands of the nascent operating system increased with each successive rollout, and
it was clear that to survive the memory on the machine had to be increased to meet
throughput requirements. By the beginning of the next decade, the HP 3000 Series
44 had made the next big jump in processing power with a significant enhancement

of the System Processing Unit (SPU) that supported up to 4 megabytes of memory. The pace of enhancements also picked up as memory doubled to eight megabytes, and the microcode that ran the computer began to be etched into the ROMs (Read Only Memory).

In the early 1960s, IBM had developed microcode to enable them to build different sized machines, all of which ran the same instruction set. This defined their successful System 360 family of machines. However, as microcode was adopted by other manufacturers, machines were designed in which the microcode became more arcane and voluminous. For the complexity of their mainframe systems, it's estimated that IBM employed somewhat over 300,000 bits of microcode.

A subsequent increase in microcode size occurred in the Digital Equipment Corporation VAX machines. VAX systems contained about 550,000 bits of microcode. This was followed by even more extensive microcode in the X86 machines based on Intel's microcomputer architecture that launched the personal computer revolution. The machine that steadily advanced personal computing by putting machines onto every office desk used around 800,000 bits of microcode. And computer complexity still continued to grow. It was the shift to the RISC architecture concepts that obviated the need for microcode and eliminated microcode complexity on the grand scale.

Following the success of the initial RISC-based machines, the first superscalar and out-of-order superscalar implementations began to be developed for RISC processors. The first superscalar RISC system, the IBM RS/6000, was introduced in the early 1990's. HP and others subsequently developed out of order superscalar implementations for their RISC architectures. Most of the RISC implementation techniques were later applied internally within the evolving X86 machines. Yet here again, hardware complexity was creeping back into the picture as the limits of these architectures were approached. All of the major RISC and X86 manufacturers have found that continued performance improvements are becoming more difficult and expensive to achieve.

At the Start: The Wide Word Project

In 1990, a project that originally was named the "Super Workstation" project, and subsequently rechristened the "PA Wide Word" effort, was inaugurated at the Hewlett-Packard laboratories. The scheduled 1989 meeting date between Frank Carrubba, Director of HP Labs, and John Young, HP CEO, to discuss initiating the project, was probably fitting for a project that was destined to send shocks through the world of processor technology. It so happened that the scheduled meeting time took place exactly when the Loma Prieta earthquake rattled California's fault lines with a sizeable trembler. Director Frank Carrubba recalled that he had just entered John Young's office when the building started to shake and ceiling tiles began to fall.

But dismissing the near natural disaster, the meeting was rescheduled and they concluded that the effort should proceed.

The project was established in HP Labs under the leadership of Dick Lampman and Bill Worley. Dick, now Director of HP Labs, served as the administrative director, and Bill acted as the technical director. Bill Worley was one of the most influential members of the design team whose work ultimately culminated in the Itanium Processor Family Architecture. He had led the development of PA-RISC from the early 1980's, and then took a leave of absence outside of HP. It was in 1989 that Frank Carrubba suggested that he be brought back to do what became the wide word project, which led to the meeting with John Young that established the project's charter.

The team's charter was, at its inception, extremely simple. Initially focused upon workstations, the core design requirements remained the same even as the scope of the project grew to encompass the broader range of products available on the market today.

- Design an advanced architecture that can move Hewlett-Packard ahead of the competition by establishing a new benchmark for speed, reliability, and ease of transition for legacy systems.
- Find ways of making machines provide superior performance by means of an innately superior architecture.
- Focus on improving the competitive performance of the workstations that work with the new architecture.
- At the same time, ensure that the design also can deliver superior price performance.

The Quadruple Conclusion of the Design Team

With this charter in mind, Bill's design team analyzed existing architectures and came to four conclusions that would prove instrumental in developing the Intel Itanium architecture. This work built upon ideas that had taken shape earlier in their work on PA-RISC, lessons learned with earlier vector and VLIW systems, and work already underway in HP Labs under Bob Rau:

1. First, that the generation beyond RISC would have to be designed explicitly to execute multiple operations in every machine cycle. Already, it was clear that there would be significant hardware complexity trying to reach this goal for RISC architectures. With the PA-RISC 8000, for example, there were over 850,000 transistors devoted just to reordering the instructions and making

some of them run in parallel. The entire previous generation PA-RISC processor chip had used only 850,000 transistors for the entire processor.

2. That there was inherent mathematical complexity in out-of-order superscalar RISC machines that would prevent them ever from sustaining over about four instruction executions per cycle in the best-case scenario. Since then, observations and testing of out-of-order superscalar type designs have validated this conclusion.

3. That for any architecture, including out-of-order superscalar RISC, the compiler explicitly must schedule instructions, in order to sustain execution of multiple instructions per cycle. This conclusion strongly implies that hardware should be kept simple, and that it should be straightforward for a compiler to schedule the concurrent execution of instructions.

4. Finally, a clean drawing board was needed in order to make the architecture scalable well beyond existing limits, while also enabling significantly simpler hardware.

With Bill Worley as the technical director, the program began to function within HP Labs. With an eye to pulling together experts in all the important critical areas, the team began to work on improving every aspect of the project's design. Silicon design, circuit design, logic design, simulation, packaging, cooling, compiler, operating system, and architecture experts all were tapped to create the new processor architecture.

Seeds of a New Partnership

By the end of 1993, Hewlett-Packard approached Intel about continuing this research as part of a partnership. It was a fortuitous time for HP to approach Intel. Given the close community of high-level designers, there was a fair amount of buzz in the air and correspondingly a lot of curiosity about what exactly was going on in HP Labs to occupy such highly qualified designers.

Additionally, the costs for building state-of-the-art silicon fabrication plants had continued to skyrocket, reaching the level of billions of dollars per plant. Rather than massive investments in HP facilities to produce the new chip, or major dependencies upon independent fabrication plants, Bill Worley had a different idea:

"In July of 1992 I proposed to the executive committee in HP Labs's annual review that what HP should do is develop our architectural ideas into a product that would become a defacto industry standard, and for that we had to partner, ideally, with a semiconductor manufacturer. At the time, we didn't know who that might be, but Intel was a premier candidate."

Certainly, this was a successful process for Intel, as it was the driving force behind building the x586 processor, known more commonly as the first generation of the Pentium. Once this field began to be mined out, it was time to focus on new ideas at the high end of the marketplace, where HP had a tremendous history of high-performance processor development expertise.

Intel's COO Paul Otellini once noted that some people in the industry "have described microprocessor architecture as the plagiarists of all time because of what they did for the first 25 years of their history—where they took every idea that they ever perceived in computer science and put it on a chip."

Complimentary Expertise and Market Forces at HP and Intel

Timing, as they say, is everything. As it turned out, the timing was right for the Itanium architecture, as the notion of collaborating on a processor that was beyond the Pentium and RISC became a unifying force for both companies. In the past, Intel's architecture design had been made with a specific goal in mind. This goal was to enable more and more capabilities for users at lower and lower costs. This was an extremely effective way to bring the benefits of standardized computing into desktops, workstations, midrange and even low-end servers.

Similarly, Hewlett-Packard was casting about for the best method to capitalize on our advanced silicon designs. The opportunity to bring the same economies of scale benefits to mainframe class replacements that had been brought to minicomputers in the prior generations was a major one. As Paul Otellini succinctly put it, Intel wanted to move 'up market', and Hewlett-Packard wanted to be able to reduce costs and take advantage of design improvements simultaneously

Intel turned out to be the ideal partner for HP in terms of interest in the product, processor architecture and design expertise, and had the ability to bring the volume design and manufacturing capabilities to bear. Given their long-term involvement in processor design, both Intel and HP got a platform with a tremendous technological pedigree. This legacy was a very attractive one for both computer buyers and application developers.

In essence, the Itanium architecture allowed HP and Intel to design a processor architecture that met the cost function, shattered the speed barrier, and remained true to the design standard of simplicity. It was this standard that led to the development of the Explicitly parallel Instruction Computing (EPIC) architecture, which we discuss in more detail in Chapter 7. The goal of EPIC architecture, as Bill Worley put it, was is to do away with all unnecessary complexity in the hardware to enable all of the transistors on the chip to contribute to performance.

Itanium as a New Processor Benchmark

With all the emphasis on bringing together the 'best and brightest' from two design giants, one might think that the process of collaboration was not only the means, but also the end. Yet nothing could be farther from the truth. The project that became the

Itanium processor was never an academic exercise, and far from being a 'blue sky' corporate myth. Instead, it was an extremely focused, conscious effort to put the brakes on cost and pare back layer upon layer of complexity that had crept into the RISC world. Most importantly, it was to bring value to the corporate purchaser at a level of performance that had never been seen in the IT world before.

To call the Itanium platform a rather big investment on both companies' part would be an understatement. Several years of diligent architecture and design work were committed to bring this to the marketplace. In some ways, it really does define what the architecture for the next decade or two will be, in part because you can only afford to do a project of this scope once every decade or two.

From the start, the Intel Itanium processor family was designed to effectively take the high ground and become an industry standard. Also, it was decided upon within the Intel and HP partnership that this new standard be one that could be produced in volume and made available to a number of computer system OEMS. This really highlights the scope of what was being attempted; normally, a revolutionary design is released in small quantities and then mass produced only as the performance features 'trickle down' to the mass audience.

Instead, for the team, top performance was pursued—but the goal was also to be the cost competitive market leader and the foundation for corporate computing and enterprise computing. This foundation was not one to last for just a year or two, but for the next several *decades*.

The Business Drivers Met by Itanium Processor Development

Intel CEO Craig Barrett sums up the most immediate benefit that companies will see from implementing the Intel Itanium architecture in their businesses by pointing to the need to process immense chunks of data. As he puts it, "None of us can escape it because the business models—the customer bases—increasingly drive us to analyze more and more information."

This ability to handle bigger databases with tremendous speed allows businesses to mine or analyze more and more data in a cost effective fashion. Arguably, the most urgent business management issue for large companies is how to really handle the huge databases that make up their product list, customer base, and order history. It's the Itanium-based systems that can take and process this vast amount of data and analyze it efficiently.

Businesses are also seeing their customer base increasingly going international. If one uses Intel or HP as a proxy, then about 70% of business now is done outside of the United States. Barrett notes that any company that follows a similar track of success will not be able to avoid dealing with customers around the world. Therefore, it will be forced to look at marketplaces around the world on a *real time basis*.

If the trend is for successful companies to go global, then it only means more customers, more complexity in the business, faster product introductions, and streamlined supply chain models. In turn, this will require more data, more instantaneous access to the data, faster analysis of the data, and faster response to the supply chain.

Envisioning the Utilization of Itanium's Power

Itanium processing power has already entered the market and is in its second generation (Itanium 2 processor) as you read this book. Yet its full impact will be some time in coming as successive processor iterations are released with better performance, and more independent software vendors port their applications to take advantage of Intel's Itanium processor. The impact from the architecture's ability to handle high volumes of data and computations faster and more reliably will be better workstations and servers, at lower cost to customers.

The following are a couple of examples of early users of the Itanium processors. These are early adopters of new technology who have big plans for their Itanium systems, as you will see by reading the case studies.

Infrastructure Savings Through the PNNL Supercomputer

With the introduction of Itanium-based servers and workstations, the pace of scientific discovery has picked up tremendously. For example, Pacific Northwest National Laboratory and the U.S. Department of Energy, partnering with Hewlett-Packard, is working on a project that will result in one of the world's most powerful Linux-based supercomputers by mid-2003.

This super computer, comprised of servers using the Itanium 2, will be used to study complex chemical problems that form the basis for new discoveries in areas such as life sciences, subsurface transport, material design, atmospheric chemistry and combustion. In addition, they will apply the supercomputer to study geochemistry and biochemistry; radioactive and chemical waste detection, storage and management; systems biology; genomics; proteomics; materials science; fundamental studies in chemistry and computer science; and catalysis.

Consisting of 1,438 Itanium-2 processors, the new HP supercomputer will have an expected total peak performance of more than 9.2 teraflops—roughly 8,300 times faster than a current personal computer. Calculations that currently take a month to complete could be done in one day on the new system.

"As we try to use computational results to replace difficult and expensive experiments, increased computational power is essential," said David Dixon, associate director of theory, modeling, and simulation at William R. Wiley Environmental Molecular Sciences Laboratory (EMSL), a DOE scientific user facility at PNNL where the supercomputer is being installed. "The advanced architecture of the HP supercomputer provides that power, which will permit us to attain close to peak performance on our key computational chemistry problems."

What makes the key difference in the speed of discoveries is the quantum leap forward in mathematical modeling made possible by the Itanium architecture. Instead of having to build infrastructure to handle tests, store material, and dispose of hazardous waste, the measurements or interactions can be modeled quickly and accurately on a computer that can handle the additional complexity. By removing the need to handle potentially volatile chemical or nuclear materials, the work done by the researchers has become much easier and safer.

Academic and Industrial Design at the University of Stuttgart

The High-Performance Computing Center at the University of Stuttgart is one of the four largest computer centers in Germany. The university utilizes a vector supercomputer, visual computer, and cluster-structured distributed computer. The center is set up with a special arrangement in which it provides computing resources for both the university and for industrial applications.

The hardware used is an Express5800/1160Xa, capable of loading 16 Intel Itanium processors. Applications include impact simulation required for the safety design of automobile companies in Germany, and computational flow analysis simulation required for the air conditioner design. The High-Performance Computing Center also provides tools and expertise for science and technology computing.

By utilizing the 64-bit addressing and 64GB large main memory capacity that the Itanium-based systems can handle, large-scale end processing can be performed. The computing time was reduced to a tenth of the time required by the previous system. Given the Itanium's advantage in handling these jobs, the fundamental calculation code can be run up to 1.5 times faster than the previous system.

These are just a few of the early examples of how the power of new Itanium systems is being deployed to improve computing on a grand scale. Several others can be found in Appendix B.

In Summary

- Early development of systems had to strike a balance between performance and the need to limit complexity. For example, growing hardware complexity in the superscalar implementations of RISC machines was successfully contained at one point by understanding how instructions were executed and how this process could be made more efficient.

- The initial goal of the design team from HP and Intel was to create an advanced architecture that could move ahead of the competition by establishing a new benchmark for speed, reliability, and ease of transition for legacy systems.

• The design team for what would become the Itanium architecture came up with four main conclusions, which formed the basis for the architecture design: The new architecture must be explicitly designed for executing multiple operations in every machine; a hard limit exists that prevents a RISC-based microprocessor from getting above the level of about four instruction executions per cycle; compilers explicitly must schedule code to sustain execution of multiple instructions per machine cycle; the new architecture had to be scalable well beyond the existing limit.

• Several factors in the business world pushed Itanium's development as well, particularly the increasing need to manage and access bigger and bigger databases with tremendous speed, allowing businesses to analyze more and more data in a cost effective fashion.

• Itanium's power will be utilized a number of ways, the earliest adopters of the technology have been the engineers and scientists who run applications for simulations that were previously solely in the realm of very large and expensive supercomputers. This trend is now extending into mission-critical applications in every enterprise.

The Next Technology Paradigm: Computing as a Utility

If you can make [computing] a utility, that means your network is on all the time...and you'll use special services only when you need them. If you do one day's work of supercomputing a month, you don't need to own it.

—Joel Birnbaum, former CTO, Hewlett-Packard Company

In This Chapter:

- Three-tier computing
- What characterizes computing as a utility
- Distributed versus centralized computing
- Effects of the growth of the Web
- Breaking the hardware cycle

Joel Birnbaum, who was HP's chief technology officer at the time, made a very telling remark when he said that Itanium does for computing what the World Wide Web did for data. That statement could be taken to mean many things to different people, but for our purposes it means two important things: first, that computing power can be easily shared among dispersed and disparate user communities in a single organization, and second, that you can treat computing power as you would gas or electric utilities—you will be allowed to pay for only what you need to use and not tie up capital in paying for a shortage or excess of what you need.

The Itanium-based system makes the perfect platform for this "utility" computing for three reasons.

1. The Intel Itanium processor family[9] has great flexibility in that it can run the three major operating systems while delivering impressive speed.
2. The incredible degree of vendor support for the architecture indicates that all major applications will be written to run on it over the next 5 years.
3. The move to utility computing may be completely enabled by Itanium due to its ability to remove incompatibility issues and provide support that is completely transparent to end users and programmers alike.

Ideas Behind Three-tier Computing

With the rise of less costly, faster, and more reliable networking software and hardware, most large enterprises organize their infrastructure on some variant of a three-tiered computing approach, outlined as follows.

First Tier

In its simplest form, computing networks today in any large enterprise environment store their data in a back-end system. This back end, or first tier, is actually where all of the data used in the organization is collected and retrieved for mining, editing, and storage. Typically, this data is organized in a large back-end database, such as the software products from Oracle,[10] Sybase, and Informix.

Second Tier

This tier is where most of the applications on the system exist, which is why it is also called the application tier. Applications on this level don't mean the desktop-centric user programs, such as Microsoft[11] Word or Excel. Instead, these are the more complex enterprise resource planning (ERP), customer resource management (CRM), and supply chain applications, accounting software, and company billing applications.

The main point is that these applications all need to interact with the data that is stored on the back end. A company uses the databases on the back end to provide the information used to interact with the applications. The application pulls the data from the back end as demanded and processes it, then puts it right back into the database as the information is modified.

---

9.   Intel and Itanium are registered trademarks or trademarks of Intel Corporation or its subsidiaries in the United States and other countries.
10.   Oracle is a registered U.S. trademark of Oracle Corporation, Redwood City, California.
11.   Microsoft is a U.S. registered trademark of Microsoft Corporation.

Third Tier

This tier is also called the *edge* of the network. Though this edge is somewhat sinister sounding, it really refers to where the company's internal network touches the network of the outer world, the vast "cloud" that is the Internet. Here is where the enterprise either branches off to users who may be widely dispersed geographically or to other companies. The edge of the network is where the firewall and the systems that handle data encryption/decryption as well as Web serving exist. A clear representation of this tiered system is seen in Figure 4–1.

Computing as a Utility

The three-tiered system is certainly one that works, but it is still centered on what kind of hardware investment an organization can make. This is why a great deal of thought during the Intel Itanium architecture development process went into how we wanted to shape computing for the decade after the millennium. The idea that came out of the lab is for a much different kind of computing capability than exists today.

The umbrella concept is to shift the idea of computing as a hardware purchase to one as a service purchase. Several original principles underlay the use of Itanium power to shift computing into this new paradigm—the paradigm of computing as a utility. Each principle was incorporated into the design capabilities of the Intel Itanium processor family.

Transparency to the End User

Transparency in this case means that the processes, the software and hardware used in the computing process, are effectively invisible to the end user. To continue in the vein of likening computing power to electricity, it is much like flipping on a

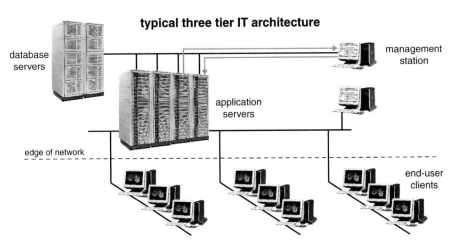

Figure 4-1 A Three-Tiered Network System

light switch. Does the average person have to know how many kilowatts are available or what model the plant generators are? Probably not—it is more likely that the person simply wants an end result, in this case the automatic application of the switch to give him or her the light that is desired in an intuitive and easy manner.

Ubiquitous Presence

The new computing model would also have to be pervasive, both in constant availability and in scope. It was decided early on at Hewlett-Packard that if we were going to pursue the development of this paradigm, we wanted to do it on a big scale to make it work on a large computer that would be very fast and scalable even from an enterprise standpoint.

HP's product family spans enough categories that the pervasive nature of what we wanted is eminently doable. The product categories available span three "capacities," including entry-level servers for departmental sharing or clustering, midrange servers for divisional or line-of-business units, and high-end enterprise servers to run the entire organization or perform heavy calculations. Each product provides leadership performance today, runs HP's version of UNIX, HPUX-11i, and offers easy upgrade features to future generations of processor technologies. The extent of the offerings at different levels is illustrated in Figure 4–2.

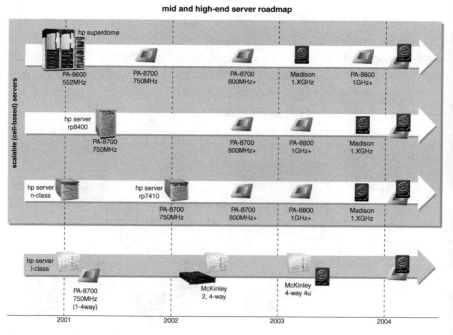

Figure 4-2   Extent and Types of Mid- and High-Level Computing

Intuitive Use

Given the pace of business today and the constant cycle of change in the technical world, there is a definite shift away from being concerned with how a given IT system works. Today, we're more likely to be concerned with what the system does to complete a task or project. So in many ways, people are already beginning to view computing power as an information utility or appliance.

An appliance, in computing terms, is a single-purpose system, usually stripped to the bare functionality necessary for it to accomplish its specific task. Appliances are widely used today for the "edge of network" servers. These are servers on which the user simply needs to encrypt or de-encrypt secure transactions that serve up Web pages to thousands of online users.

Ability to Handle Mixed Networks

A final principle for the computing utility concept was the ability to handle a mixed network—to work with many of the operating systems that you can find in the corporate or scientific world, as seen in Figure 4-3.

The Pendulum Swing of Distributed Computing Versus Centralized Computing

Given the ideas that we wanted to offer for the next generation of computing power, it's worth asking, Why did HP decide to pursue the concept of computing as a utility? There are two main reasons for this shift: the move back toward the idea of central computing management and the growth of the World Wide Web and its

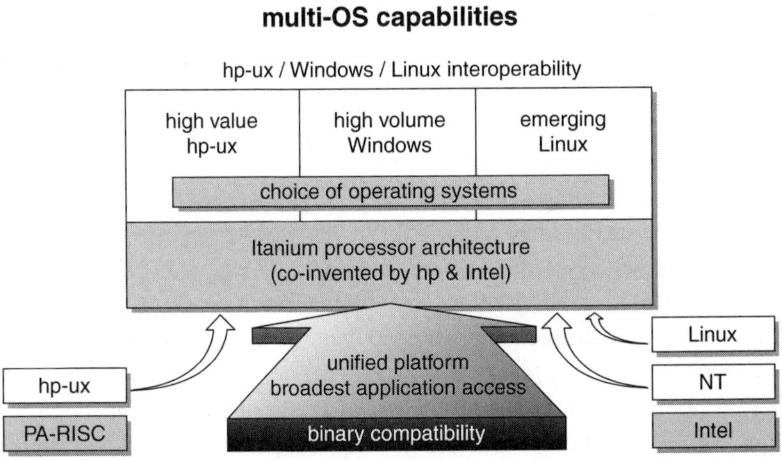

multi-OS capabilities

hp-ux / Windows / Linux interoperability

| high value hp-ux | high volume Windows | emerging Linux |

choice of operating systems

Itanium processor architecture (co-invented by hp & Intel)

unified platform
broadest application access
binary compatibility

hp-ux
PA-RISC

Linux
NT
Intel

Figure 4-3   Different Operating Systems

attendant shift of users' perceptions about where their computing dollars can be spent. It's worth exploring both of these ideas in more detail.

Curiously, the mainstream idea about how to make computing power available to an organization swings back and forth like a pendulum between two models. At one end of the spectrum is the distributed computing idea, which spreads processing power out among as many machines as possible. On the other is the idea that it is better to centralize everything in one large machine for efficiency and ease of administration. This cycle is primarily driven by developments in technology.

In the 1970's, mainframes ran the vast bulk of computing power available. In fact, companies even ran on a more centralized business model. Since personal computers did not exist until 1981, users were restricted to access over a slower networking link via terminals. But with the rise of personal computers in the 1980's the pendulum swung the other way towards what we now call distributed computing. Eventually, the idea that you could replace one large machine with a lot of smaller machines became popular. This was the genesis of the cluster concept that we still use today by combining several small machines to work like one large one. In fact, the furthest outgrowth of this trend shows up in what is called *cooperative computing,* where the cycles on many different machines run simultaneously across the network.

The genesis of this trend truly began in 1984 when the PC–Mac wars started in earnest. The development of relatively inexpensive and reliable desktop computers moved many of the utilities that had previously been restricted to the mainframe directly onto the user's workstation. Only when the limitations of chip development came about due to Moore's second law (discussed in detail in Chapter 6) did another movement commence in the IT community.

PC Center of Expertise

By the late 1990's, these limitations led to a program at HP called the *PC Center of Expertise,* or PC-COE. We still use this term and follow the processes developed under this program. Several other large companies adopted similar plans. Under this idea, companies tried to reduce some of the technical complexity and difficulty in managing distributed computing power in their enterprises. During this time, enterprises were looking for better ways to manage the thousands of PCs on users' desks. Software and hardware upgrades and maintenance costs were spiraling out of control. HP developed an internal set of programs that run on both the users' PCs and the central server to better manage all of the computing resources in an enterprise.

To control and administer all of an organization's PCs, it was standard to have an *image* on each machine to indicate what applications can be run and supported. This decision was usually made for easier support and training services.

Today's Trend: Server Consolidation

The trend today in the first decade of the new millennium is to move to server consolidation. This shift towards consolidating all of the computing functionality into one place is motivated by a need to reduce the complexity of the IT infrastructure, which by now could have several different servers, each handling unique applications. Reducing the physical distribution of the machines before consolidation also makes the system easier to manage.

Imposing standards on different, relatively standalone desktop PCs simply could not match the inherent efficiency in having computing power administered from a single physical access point. Today, many companies are looking at how to consolidate applications distributed across many servers onto one single machine. This is the reason IBM put Linux[12] on a mainframe: to attempt to consolidate all Linux applications onto a single server and to get better utilization out of its mainframe installed base.

This drive to consolidate points to the fact that all computing is becoming more a utility; instead of granting users even more powerful asset control (more expensive desktop PCs), organizations are trying to get users to draw their data and in some cases, applications, from a central server only when needed. New features in high-end servers and operating systems will eventually partition a very large server so that applications can run on different operating systems on the same machine. Now we are starting to approach the central "computing generator" of an information utility.

Future HP servers like today's HP Superdome, with its cell structure, will run a specific operating system and its applications within an individual partition. Partitioning allows you to divide up the machine's computing system so that a single machine can run as two or more machines. Rather than having a bunch of physical machines to divide up the work done on different operating systems and applications, all of the work can be done on one machine. For example, if you have 32 processors, you can allocate 16 to run UNIX,[13] 8 to run Windows, and the rest to run Linux. This can make system usage very efficient.

The Growth of the Web

The growth of the Internet is other key breakthrough in the area of treating computing as a service and utility as opposed to an infrastructure investment. Once again, there are several reasons for this. The Internet provides:

12. Linux is a registered trademark of Linus Torvalds.
13. UNIX is a registered trademark of The Open Group.

- a large, cost-effective network.
- a delivery mechanism to deliver information to people anywhere.
- a delivery mechanism to deliver computing power to people anywhere.

The last two points are perhaps the deepest and most critical. The idea of the improved networking ability to provide a delivery mechanism allows a user to do more and more tasks that are not connected with the box sitting on his or her desktop. This in turn enables people to look at computing as a service (What can I do online to get a project completed?) as opposed to a capital investment (a bigger box on a desk). This idea is enhanced by the fact that an Itanium-based system can run the three major operating systems on the same platform and still deliver great performance.

In short, the growth of the Internet showed that PCs suffer from serious limitations. A personal computer can hold only so much data and so much memory, and if you really want to access more information, it is now impossible to do so without a network connection. The connection allows you to access information that simply can't be stored on a PC and allows you to interface with larger databases and more complex applications.

Breaking the IT Hardware Spiral

A final aspect of utility computing is that a major capital investment is not necessarily a prerequisite for getting high levels of computing power. In fact, laying out large amounts of capital to buy needed computing capacity may in itself be obsolete soon.

Instead, you should be able to buy computing power the way you do electricity or water. If your needs spike up or drop down, you should be able to buy more or less in a given year or month as needed. Computing as a utility should foster the paradigms of pay by use, don't worry where the work is done, and it doesn't matter what kind of machine the work is done on so long as it is fast and accurate.

Most clients agree that this model will become increasingly attractive in the coming months or years. It helps lift IT departments out of the insane spiral of hardware obsolescence that afflicts both companies and home users alike. You've experienced this spiral of obsolescence if you've ever purchased a computer. By the time you buy and install it, you realize that it's almost obsolete! The answer to this is a system on which you can keep the interface, keyboard, and monitor you're comfortable with and stop worrying about hardware.

By taking this approach, you free up entire IT departments' spending cycle. The cycle of investing in new hardware every 2 to 3 years ends immediately. Instead, buying computing power is keyed to your demand, as you would purchase electrical power or water. If you think about the computing power as electricity idea, the analogy can be carried even further.

- The generation of electricity = Large enterprise-class cell-based systems such as HP's Superdome server
- The transportation of electricity = The Internet or a companies' intranet
- The distribution of electricity = The company's local area network on a site or campus

Your company becomes more a distribution point, the spigot for computing power that can be turned on or off according to need. It may not be long before companies can pay their computing bill in the same way they pay for other utilities today. And the idea is to bring this to thousands, hundred of thousands, and then millions of users who can also buy computing power as needed.

In Summary

- In today's world, many large enterprises rely on a three-tiered system of network architecture: back-end servers that hold data, application servers that process this data, and edge-of-the-network servers that act as guides and guard for data traffic going in and out.
- Computing as a utility would change this, primarily because it would be more pervasive and intuitive, and would provide more flexible, as-needed coverage.
- The first major contributor to this idea is the current swing towards server consolidation.
- The second contributor is the growth of the Internet, which has made networking more ubiquitous, easier, less costly, and faster.
- Computing as a utility means no more large capital investments in applications for each user every 2 or 3 years. Users can keep the workstation while the server supplies updated applications and data storage. This concept allows you to purchase only the amount of power you need, much as you purchase electricity.

The Itanium Adoption Curve

"Commercial customers accept new technology when it's 'proven to be proven'. High performance technical computing is the way to prove out to this market segment that it's time to move into a new world of performance."

—from HP Presentation on Technical Computing

In this Chapter:

• Adoption Curve—A Recognized Phenomenon

• Early Adopters and the Early Majority

• High Performance Technical Computing

• The Importance of Floating Point Mathematics

• Itanium-based platform will quickly take over Technical Computing Environments

Traditionally, there's been a 'cascade' effect whenever a new microprocessor architecture is introduced in the computing world. We've seen time and again that releasing a new product that promises a forward leap in term of performance will be eagerly seized upon by the users with the most critical problems to solve. From there it's only a short time before the adoption spreads into other areas. This spread increases exponentially as more and more user segments come into the fold, starting as a trickle and then into a cascading flood of adoption.

Similarly, where Itanium[14]-based systems are first used in the market depends on how central the dual needs of performance and the need to use a wide range of applications are to the solving a company's problems. We have already seen a rapid adoption by the technical market segments where the performance need is most critical and many of the application vendors have already embraced the architecture.

The widespread adoption of Itanium-based platform in the main commercial segments will quickly follow suit as it is proven to be the best architecture by the most demanding early users. Continued success of additional members of the Intel® Itanium® processor family® is sure to follow, as the chip series is designed to anticipate and support the ever-increasing demands for computation in the age of the Internet.

Adoption Curve—A Recognized Phenomenon

In the past, we've seen that the first to adopt new technology are the customers that require pure performance—those in the 'hard' sciences such as physics and chemistry. The next group to latch on to a new system may be the remaining high performance users that may be more cost conscious or dependent on third party applications—those in engineering and industrial design. Then clients such as financial traders look at the performance gains made by the scientists and engineers and realize that the same technology will make a blinding fast workstation do equally fast trading and market analysis. At that point, it is only a matter of time before more widespread interest is achieved as more customers show interest for the new technology.

By any standard, the Itanium architecture is a new technology that affects performance in a fundamental way. When you change something that is at the core of the performance equation, it creates an opportunity that is irresistible to those 'early adopters' who love new technology and don't mind being first. The Itanium processor family's acceptance hinges on how these early adopters prove out the chip and decide where to use it. The largest segment of clients, the 'commercial mainstream' tend to wait until the new technology is proven. Given the size of the market that 'commercial clients' make up, as seen in Figure 5-1, in the end it is this market that makes Itanium-based system purchases on a scale that justifies the investment in new chip architecture.

For the Itanium-based systems' development, Hewlett-Packard went out and performed interviews with end users and focus groups. The customers from the

---

14.   Intel and Itanium are registered trademarks or trademarks of Intel Corporation or its subsidiaries in the United States and other countries.

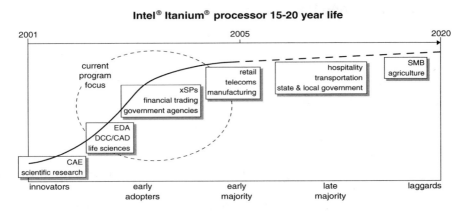

Figure 5-1 The Projected Itanium Adoption Curve Among Different User Segments

commercial segment—financial trading, bankers, manufacturing, and retail all said the same thing when it came to adoption of new technology. They all expressed interest in what the chip could do—but they didn't want to be the first on the block to have it. It was imperative to see someone else use it first.

Due to this innate conservatism, Itanium, like all new processor families, is more appealing to customers with critical needs that can be addressed immediately with the technology. Where price performance improvements are two times or greater running the same applications, they're willing to work with early technology because they stand to gain the most from the improved performance.

From this early user segment, other customers that may be more risk averse watch closely and wait for their key applications to move to the new architecture with proven performance gains and system stability. What's more, early adopters such as scientists can add legitimacy to the Itanium-based platform as they push the limits of the architecture in ways that other business or design users might not.

This cycle has repeated itself more than a few times in Hewlett-Packard's history. Most recently, we've seen that very same adoption curve when firms moved to the RISC processor. The technical market adopts the latest and greatest from the labs for an immediate performance boost and the market adoption spills quickly into the commercial segments. It's a form of legitimacy for a new architecture to work so well that the more cautious clients can look and say, 'it's working for them, I have to have it or I'll be left behind.'

Early Adopters and the Early Majority

Early Adopters and the Early Majority are both parts of the same general customer segment—that of the clients who want to get in on the earliest phases of Itanium adoption. (See Figure 5-1, above.) What separates an Early Adopter from an Early Majority? It stems from the nature of the problem facing the user. As a general rule, Early Adopters fit the following profile:

- Early adopters are doing the experiments that require Itanium to be pushed to its full potential.
- Early Adopters are comprised of people who want or need to get ahead of the technology curve.
- Early adopters have an intensive, immediate need for a level of computing power that is a full magnitude above what they have available.
- Early Adopters normally include science and research laboratories that work with highly complex mathematical models.

Because an Early Adopter's problems are so complex and computer intensive they just live with the fact that it can take a week or even a month to run a single problem! If you're in such an unenviable position, then anyone who claims to have something that cuts the wait time down to a week or a day is nothing short of a godsend. That's an amazing performance gain that can be received in no other way.

What's more, if the performance gain can be had for a reasonable price, it's icing on the cake. Early Adopters, by their very nature, will go through whatever it takes to adopt the technology because of the extreme need.

Users in Early Majority are technically in the same market segment. However, there's a subtle but immediately discernable difference between the two groups. Early Majority users tend to follow the profile outlined below:

- They include government agencies and laboratories running theoretical models.
- A slightly lower priority is placed on performance and precision, if only because the nature of the problems can be handled moderately well on existing equipment.
- A fifty to one hundred percent gain in performance is considered extremely valuable, especially if it can be done without a major price gain.

In essence, problems faced by customers in the Early Majority are not so critical that they're jumping at any solution immediately. Itanium power is clearly desired, but not to the degree that they need to be at the front of the line with the Early Adopters.

High Performance Technical Computing

No matter their differences in performance of Itanium adoption, Early Adopters and Early Majority users can be grouped together in the type of computing that is being performed. This is High Performance Technical Computing, (HPTC for short), and it's best described as any form of computing where you are using the mathematical, analytical power of the processor.

The focus is on mathematical precision such as the multiplication of very large or small numbers with long numbers of decimal places and trying to get the solution in a speedy manner. Another way to describe it is in term of complexity: Illustrating a Windows background is not HPTC, but Pixar-style digital content creation is. Using Microsoft[15] Paint would not count as processor intensive for HPTC, but drafting designs of industrial equipment in a major vendor's CAD application certainly would.

The people performing technical computing are the ones who use computer cycles in gross quantities. The case studies done by the National Crash Analysis Center, (NCAC), in Washington is a great example of the demands that HPTC can place on a computer system. If you're going to simulate the crash of a couple of cars, you'll be looking at every minute element of the subject matter as it changes and goes through the crash test.

On current RISC based technology, this is a simulation that runs for an extremely long time to get the data crunched. According to one of the team members at the NCAC, on a 3-4 year old server it takes a solid month to run a single crash analysis. He got an Itanium based system in place and the exact same crash analysis reduced the calculation time to less than 48 hours.

NCAC is a typical high performance, technical computing client. They have problems that can be run today, but take extremely long run times. In the past, these clients might require a supercomputer to run these problems. However, even if they are one of the lucky few that can get access to one, using Itanium-based systems to work through these problems provides a much less expensive alternative.

It also illustrates how when computing power is available at a superior price-performance ratio, the additional power is immediately re-directed at solving more complex problems. In the case of NCAC, once it became less time-intensive to work on a single, straightforward head-on crash, they began to expand their work into more difficult studies.

For example, testing how off-center crashes might be simulated, or the multiple impacts of a car that collides with an object and then goes off the road. The addi-

15.   Microsoft is a U.S. Registered trademark of Microsoft Corp.

tional power of the Itanium-based system allows them to more closely simulate a real-world problem. The end result is that we'll be driving safer cars in the future.

Importance of Itanium Floating Point Performance

When working with mathematical equations, such as the kind found in high-energy physics, fluid dynamics, and weather simulations, to say that the equations become complex is to seriously understate the case. Luckily for Itanium-based systems users, the registers and other elements of the chip were designed to optimize the Itanium processor family's ability to perform floating-point calculations.

In complex simulations such as weather or fluid dynamics, there are so many variables that few if any organizations outside of government research centers have really tried to pursue an effective, highly accurate simulation. This is the domain of the people who practice HPTC, and is where floating-point performance is most useful.

'Floating point' calculations are so called because they deal with equations where the decimal 'floats' around. For example, multiplying an integer that extends to 10 decimal places by another integer that is extended out to the 10th power.

Floating point performance is concerned with the places that go beyond the decimal. This capability is absolutely necessary when pinpoint accuracy is needed, such as in delicate scientific experiments. There are two critical elements involving how many decimal places of precision the computer can deal with in order to give you the most exact answer possible.

Extending the Decimal

The first important element needed to get the precision needed in many of these calculations is to be able to handle the largest number of decimal places possible. The more levels of decimal point accuracy available, the more precise the answer. For example, a 64-bit wide number that an Itanium-based system can handle obviously holds many more levels of precision than a 32-bit wide number used by RISC machines.

Reducing Rounding Error

The second element deals with the small, incremental errors that are inevitable when limitations are placed on the number of digits that are available on the machine performing the calculations. While incremental errors by themselves can be microscopically small, taken cumulatively they can throw the off the final solution.

A common example is where you want to multiply two decimal numbers with long strings of digits. You'll get what's called 'round off' error. Let's say that you're working with one number that runs out to five digits beyond the decimal point and a second number that has eight or nine digits beyond the decimal point.

However, your computer may only be able to hold a number that goes out to six decimal places. In order to arrive at a solution, the computer 'rounds' off the back end of the number.

When doing equations that require precision, you don't want to 'drop' those extra digits. If you're performing millions and millions of calculations, you'll end up with a cumulatively great error. And of course, you'll come to a wrong conclusion from the erroneous data given back to you.

Built into the Intel Itanium processor is a math function that can help with these types of calculations. This function actually provides a couple of extra bits within the function to increase the precision of the final answer. Many HPTC applications take advantage of the fact that this instruction is there, as this gives better accuracy and the performance to execute this kind of math.

Itanium Growth in Technical Computing

Technical computing in and of itself can be done on a wide range of systems, as illustrated in Figure 5-2. At the base level, there are systems that contain only one or two CPUs and are used by the engineers doing Computer Aided Engineering (CAE) tasks. Today, Hewlett-Packard offers Itanium-based systems consisting of 2-CPU workstatiopns and 4-CPU symmetrical multi-processing (SMP) systems.

At the higher end you see the processing power of a cluster of computers to act as one big computer. The UNIX[16] and Linux[17] world works this very well. A cluster can focus the power of smaller computers to create a sort of supercomputer.

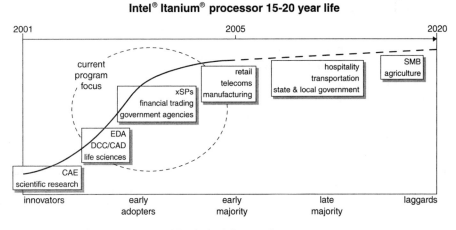

Figure 5-2 Different Levels of Technical Computing

16. UNIX is a U.S. registered trademark of The Open Group.
17. Linux is a registered trademark of Linus Torvalds.

"HP-UX Clustering" is the name we give for production-oriented clusters that supply enterprises with compute and storage resources.

These are normally—but not always—"mid-range" devices that contain tens of processors. Typically they are used for production-oriented customers who need the robustness of HP-UX and the availability features that HP-UX provides. Prime examples in this arena include aerospace and automobile manufacturers.

Another option available is what we call "Native Linux Clustering". This is the term for those who normally are the higher-end clusters found often in science and research laboratories. These customers tend to be more price-conscious, more leading-edge customers who are more likely to do their own intense system administration and system integration.

The next boost involves the clustering itself. High-end research institutes are looking more and more to these computing clusters to maximize their price: performance ratio. For these two reasons alone, 95% of HPTC buyers purchased Linux or UNIX-based systems in 2002.

And finally, the last increase in performance comes directly from the Itanium chip's built in ability to handle floating-point equations with extra precision and performance.

Itanium Will Quickly Spread into Technical Computing Environments

While predictions of the speed and steepness of an adoption curve are always tricky, it's at least more of a science than an art, as there are historical trends to look back upon. HPTC is a market segment that embraces change for the reasons outlined in this chapter, and our goal is to move people working with HPTC from RISC-based system to Itanium-based systems in no more than two to three years.

If you look at Figure 5-3, you'll see that Itanium-based system orders in the HPTC market are predicted to surpass RISC systems in 2003, tracking Itanium availability in midrange and enterprise platforms.

We're predicting that Intel Itanium processors in the high end of the market will take over from RISC processors as early as 2004. And, of course, the impact in the market doesn't stop there, or even with the 'cascade' effect across the early adopters and early majority. Over time, the same kind of power will cascade down to the level of individual desktop computers. At that point, it gets even more interesting, and the subject of a fair amount of speculation discussed in Part 4 of this book.

servers sold for technical computing applications

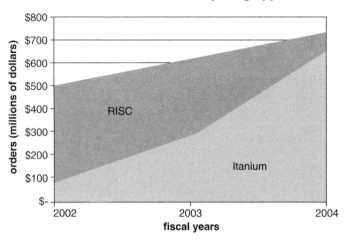

Figure 5-3 Market Sales of RISC versus Itanium Architecture

In Summary

- HP recognizes that there is a 'curve' to the speed of a new product's adoption. Often times, it's defined by the willingness of the Early Adopter and Early Majority segments to take on a new technology. Only after the technology is proven will the mass market follow.
- The difference between the two crucial segments of Early Adopters and the Early Majority lies in how critical their needs are for computing power. Early Adopters tend to be in the fields of science and research, while Early Majority users are typically in the more commercial fields such as Telecommunications, Financial Services and Manufacturing.
- High Performance Technical Computing (HPTC) is the kind of intense, heavy math based computing that is done by most Early Adopters.
- Itanium-based systems are ideally suited for conquering HPTC needs due to their ability to handle Floating Point mathematics with performance and precision. This speed and precision comes from the ability to handle 64-bit numbers and to reduce 'rounding error'.
- Itanium-based systems adoption is predicted to spread into Technical Computing Environments at a rapid pace, outselling RISC beginning in 2003 or 2004.

How Itanium Architecture Upholds Moore's First Law While Suspending Moore's Second Law

"Moore's Law is important because it is the only stable ruler we have today...It's a sort of technological barometer. It very clearly tells you that if you take the information processing power you have today and multiply by two, that will be what your competition will be doing 18 months from now. And that is where you too will have to be."
—Michael Malone, "Chips Triumphant," *Forbes ASAP*, February 1996.

In this Chapter:

- Semiconductor Costs
- Moore's First Law Examined
- Moore's Second Law Examined
- Determining Factors for the Second Law: Manufacturing Capability and Costs
- Suspending Moore's Second Law via Itanium Processor Family

Gordon Moore, the former Director of the R&D Laboratories at Fairchild Semiconductor and co-founder of Intel®[18], once said that "there is no room left to squeeze anything out by being clever. Going forward from here we have to depend on the two size factors—bigger dice and finer dimensions." He was referring to an

---

18.   Intel and Itanium are registered trademarks or trademarks of Intel Corporation or its subsidiaries in the United States and other countries.

impending limitation on the number of transistors one can place on a microchip. Up to this point, there had been an exponential growth in the density and number of transistors placed on the chip.

Increasing the number of transistors on a chip allows you to create more powerful machines. However, increasing the number of transistors on what is essentially the same amount of chip 'real estate' requires manufacturers to continue shrinking the size of the transistors. In turn, this steady reduction in size will increase the cost of building such microprocessors. Moore's pronouncement was a warning that the continued growth of computing power and the reduction of its cost could soon be in for a significant slowdown.

Semiconductor Functions and Costs

Semiconductors, which are also known as computer microchips or integrated circuits, contain numerous electrical pathways that connect transistors with other electronic components. Transistors act to store information on the semiconductor, by holding an electrical charge or by holding little or no charge.

Today's computer chips are almost entirely built on silicon wafers because silicon has the chemical properties that allow it to either conduct electricity or be converted to a conduction insulator. Silicon itself remains inexpensive and abundant as the fabrication wafers used are made of highly purified, refined sand. It is the precision required in the manufacturing process and not the raw material that contains all but a fraction of the cost and the added value.

The cost of the semiconductor itself is measured in two dimensions: complexity and size. Historically, as the size of the circuit decreases, so has the cost. This declining cost curve of the semiconductor has made the mass production and sale of computing devices.

Moore's First Law

Gordon Moore observed that the number of transistors that could be placed on a microchip to populate a silicon-based integrated circuit would double every couple of years. Though initially an obscure treatise on the growth of computing power through more precise manufacturing techniques, the media dubbed the equation "Moore's Law." Moore's observation shows that when plotted out, an exponential growth curve in transistor density resulting in increased performance and decreased cost per unit. It was also translated into a general 'rule of thumb' among IT professionals that on average, computing power would double ever eighteen months.

This prediction has been on track so far. As the chart below indicates, the growth in the number of transistors has been substantial, roughly doubling every couple of years. The complexity of the calculations, breadth of applications, and amount of data that can be handled by the IT infrastructure has followed suit.

	Year of introduction	Transistors
4004	1971	2,250
8008	1972	2,500
8080	1974	5,000
8086	1978	29,000
286	1982	120,000
386™ processor	1985	275,000
486™ DX processor	1989	1,180,000
Pentium® processor	1993	3,100,000
Pentium II processor	1997	7,500,000
Pentium III processor	1999	24,000,000
Pentium 4 processor	2000	42,000,000

Moore's Second Law

Gordon Moore continued to follow up on the progress of the microchip, when he began to see a new, non-technological reason that the spectacular gains reaped under the first law could be unsustainable. Essentially, the improvements in microprocessor power over the last decade or two have come from the fact that we've been able to improve the manufacturing process of putting more transistors on a single chip.

Shrinking the chip die and other sorts of 'cleverness' has done this, as Moore might say. However, Moore's follow up comes, surprisingly enough, from the field of economics: that the cost of building plants to create continually more powerful processors will continue to grow at such a rate that to depend on the doubling of power every 18-24 months due to process improvements will not be possible indefinitely.

Manufacturing Ultimately Drives Moore's First Law

The follow up to this conclusion is that as you continue to shrink the process—getting fine and finer line tracings and so on—the equipment need to control this and make it happen needs to get more and more precise. Which in turn means that each generation of manufacturing machines will cost more than the prior one.

For example, at HP we've shifted from using light to ultraviolet light to try to get better resolution on making the chip traces. This is because ultraviolet light has a shorter wavelength, allowing you to more accurately measure and produce these traces. Whenever you make a major shift to change and improve the line widths that you can produce on the chip, you basically have to build an entire new factory.

In fact, chipmakers must continually invest in new technologies. Consider that in 2000, chipmakers were building circuits 180 nanometers wide. To put that in perspective, you could line up 500 of these circuits and they would just fit across a human hair. By 2010, the industry standard is predicted to be an even more amazing 45 nanometers wide.

The entire field of semiconductor manufacturers is running into a barrier that exists in no other technological field, with the possible exception of those designing electron microscopes: the limits of optical lithography. In the normal manufacturing process, light beams are used to trace out the patterns of circuits. However, it may well be that soon even ultraviolet wavelengths are reaching a point where it's difficult to build lenses to work with the equipment effectively.

Gordon Moore postulates that eventually as manufacturers move away from optical lithography, the subsequent technique to employ in order to continue making progress that sustains the first law is the use of even shorter wavelength X-rays.

Most of the time, those outside of the semiconductor industry are amazed to hear this. True, chip making is at its base a manufacturing process, albeit a highly technical one. However, it's much different than an automobile assembly line. On an auto production line, the tolerances between designs—how well pieces fit together—are usually not measured in microns.

Shifting a plant from using Type A door to Type B hatch is normally not much of an issue. That being the case, plants can shift from building lower selling types of compact cars and change over to manufacture higher volume sport-utility vehicles in a matter of days or even hours. Contrast that with the high R&D costs for testing and building all new equipment to measure out and build chips that may be trying to cram more than double the number of transistors on a microprocessor. You start to see why changeover isn't quite as easy at it would be for a number of industrial processes.

Fab Plant Sticker Shock

In 1966, the cost for building a semiconductor fabrication plant—also called the 'tab for a fab' topped $14 million dollars. By 1995, an up-to-date plant could cost almost $1 billion. Each generation of plants requires more exotic and precise equipment to develop and turn out large numbers of the next generation of microprocessors.

Under Moore's Second Law, the general rule is that the cost of creating new, up to date manufacturing facilities doubles every generation. In the late 1980s, billion-dollar plants seemed almost inconceivable. However, at this point in time Intel alone has two plants under construction that will cost more than $2.5 billion apiece.

Fabrication development people try to reutilize as much of the previous generation's equipment as possible. However, even with the increasing number of joint ventures—much like our own with Intel—the building of a new plant remains one of the largest outlays of capital of any business field. Under Moore's second law, by 2005 the cost for a fab plant could be up as high as $10 billion.

As can be seen in Figure 6-1, the price of constructing a plant to build the processors (also known as a 'fab' plant) has soared far beyond the cost curve of any industry when it is building a new piece of equipment.

Therefore, the decision to build a plant that upholds Moore's first law of increasing processor power is one that is linked at the hip to the Second Law. If the return on investment is not there to justify spending on the scale that the Second Law demands, the first one will not be upheld. Place yourself in the position of a manufacturer like Intel—if you're going to spend $4 billion on a factory and you make 100 million chips, you know how to price accordingly to get the return by selling on the mass market. But what if you can only make 10 million chips? This may not be Intel's dilemma, but it is the problem facing every other manufacturer of their own proprietary chips.

Therefore, results of Moore's First Law are only *directly* dependent on the number of transistors on a microchip. When looked at with a slightly wider lens, it's apparent that what the results are linked to are the ability to make more sophisticated manufacturing plants economically feasible in the 18-24 month time span. The true

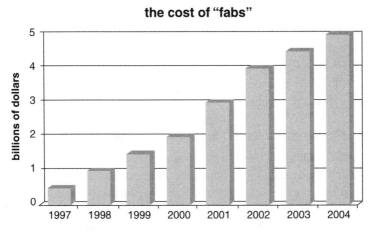

Figure 6-1 The Astronomical Rise in the Cost to Construct a Fab Plant

dependency hangs on whether or not a manufacturer like IBM, Hewlett-Packard, or Intel had the financial and technical know-how and stamina to be able to continue building new and improved plants to churn out these faster chips.

Suspending Moore's Second Law—The Battle Plan

When designing the Explicitly Parallel Instruction Computing, (EPIC) architecture, we realized early on that we could overcome Moore's second law by attacking the problem on two sides—one economic and one technical. The first, economic-approach was to create an industry standard that could bring the economies of scale that would be needed to keep the price portion of the equation in check. The second approach was to use technological advancement to uphold the levels of performance dictated by Moore's First law without doing so by doing more than changing the manufacturing process. (I.e., clever design)

The Primary Thrust: An Industry Standard

One of the reasons that HP joined forces with its supplier Intel was this law of economics. Hewlett-Packard realized that in order to create these chips cost effectively and to sell them at a reasonable price, they had to be mass-produced. But even so, the cost of the undertaking was staggering, even for a company of HP's size. However, Intel had the know-how and the manufacturing muscle to get a new architecture to the market in economically feasible numbers.

This is a key point in the way that the new design was brought to the market. On one hand, the emphasis on error correction and explicit parallelism would win acclaim in the reliability and performance arenas. However, it also needed to become an 'industry standard to achieve an optimal price-performance signature.

We were focused on this price-performance model because our end destination was not only to bring a next generation chip family to the market, but also do so in a way that would allow it to be pervasive within the market. Instead of being the 'Rolls Royce' of processors—powerful but expensive enough to only appeal to a few players—we were looking at capturing a larger audience. To go beyond the customer set of the early adopters and raise the bar not only in speed, but also in its ability to stake out and be highly successful in its market segment.

The Flanking Maneuver: Emphasize Architecture

The second approach was to get a long-term performance gain so a manufacturer wouldn't continually have to invest in only one mechanism – increasing frequency to achieve performance gains. Considering how often this was being done, we needed something that could take us (to appropriate a managing cliché) "outside of the box". Instead of relying solely on shrinking the line size or frequency alone on the chip, HP and Intel co-developed EPIC as an architectural breakthrough. This approach does not directly repeal Moore's second law, but it creates another path to performance improvements by invoking the use of software (e.g., compiler technology) to provide continual gains on top of the manufacturing breakthroughs that can apply to any architecture.

Fundamentally, the use of EPIC is a more extensible form of performance gain. Gains continue to accumulate for Itanium and its developing processor family as more and more things are done within the new architecture. In other words, moving us to a place where more things are done in parallel.

In Summary

- Semiconductor costs are not tied into their raw materials, as the silicon itself remains an inexpensive form of highly purified, refined sand. The costs come from the sophisticated machines that can meet the level of precision required in the manufacturing process.
- The ultimate cost of the semiconductor itself is measured in two dimensions: complexity and size.
- Moore's First Law states that the numbers of transistors on a chip will double every 18-24 months, hence the amount of computing power available will also double in this timeframe. Time has proven Gordon Moore's initial prediction as a correct one.
- Surprisingly enough, Moore's second law is economic: that the cost of building plants to create continually more powerful processors requires that there is sufficient market potential to support the costs. An industry standard microprocessor available to all is one way to achieve this.
- EPIC, in the form of the Itanium processor family, suspends Moore's Second Law via a business partnership that allows for excellent economy of scale, and adds, as a bonus, performance gains from a new chip architecture.

EPIC—The Appropriate Name for a Breakthrough in Processor Architecture

"Hewlett Packard was very involved with RISC, and that led to the development with Intel of this architecture called EPIC. And then from EPIC, Intel drew the blueprint and built the chip, now HP is building the systems. Kind of like the architects and the builders working together if you will..."
—Mark Hudson, HP Marketing Director

In this Chapter:

- EPIC is different than RISC
- RISC's Limitations in Parallel Processing
- Squaring Overhead
- Explicit Parallelism
- Itanium Register Set Model
- Floating Point Architecture

When you talk about an architecture, you're really discussing how the microprocessor itself is organized. With Intel, we developed an 'instruction set architecture' (ISA). Out of this collaboration on the architecture we call EPIC comes the set of instructions as to whether an application should branch at one point, load from memory at another. Thus, the best way to think about an architecture is as the boundary between hardware and software—the hardware being what gets put on the chip, and the software that which controls it.

EPIC's Break From RISC

EPIC is not an evolutionary 'extension' of RISC. In fact, it's a break from the RISC away of doing things.

As opposed to RISC, (Reduced Instruction Set Computing), the new EPIC stands for 'Explicitly Parallel Instruction Computing.' True to its name, the key difference between the two forms of architecture is that EPIC allows the computer to run more instructions at the same time—i.e., in parallel. By completing more than one instruction per CPU clock cycle, there's a corresponding gain in speed, as if you had invested in a much faster processor.

The standard method of speeding up a processor is to turn up the clock speed. The designers enable this by shrinking the distance between components, shrinking the line size on the die, and so on. However, if you're able to do two, three or even four instructions per clock cycle, you've increased your speed by a factor of two hundred, three hundred, or even four hundred percent.

Untapped Parallelism in RISC

Most of the RISC machines today are what we call '4-issue' processors. This means that in theory they can do a maximum of four things in parallel. However, because of the way the architecture of processor is set up—the hardware on the chip, and the software that controls it—this level of parallelism is rarely reached on a regular basis.

All CISC and RISC-based machines are based on the model of a Von Neumann engine. This engine is the basic computer model where the processing must appear to be done sequentially. One instruction is completed, and only then is the next picked up, and so on and so forth. It's a purely sequential architecture, and because it is set up like that, it's difficult to do anything in parallel. So you're left with a limited ability to parallelize the operations within an application.

What was done in developing an out-of-order execution RISC processor was to place control logic on the chip itself to encourage parallel running. However, in actual practice, the parallel capabilities are limited. You're left with a very basic, straight-line sequential way of doing things where more than half the processor's power is left untapped during each clock cycle. This untapped potential exists, no matter how fast your clock speed is. A graphic depiction of this is shown in Figure 7-1, shown below.

Squaring the Overhead in RISC

Additionally, we also ran into an interesting result as we tried to move beyond 4-issue machines to 6 or 8 issue machines. The overhead that was placed on the chip's

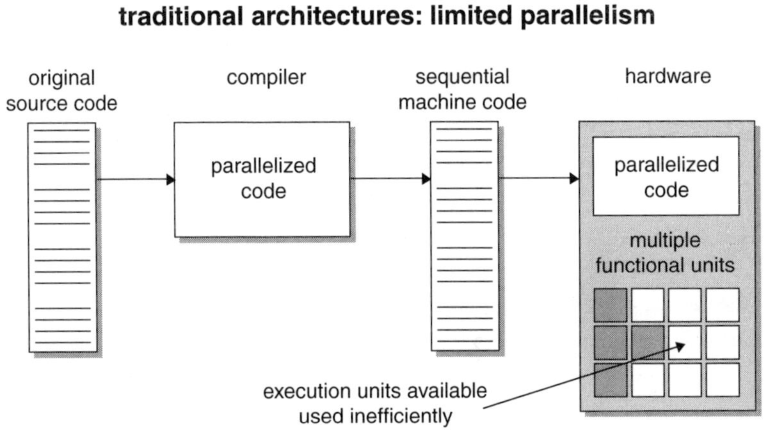

traditional architectures: limited parallelism

| original source code | compiler | sequential machine code | hardware |

parallelized code

parallelized code

multiple functional units

execution units available
used inefficiently

Figure 7-1   Traditional Architectures: Limited Parallelism

transistors just to keep track of what was going on when scheduling parallel operations increased exponentially as we increased linearly the number of functional units. Therefore, if you tried to move from a 4-issue to an 8-issue processor, the overhead did not increase by a factor of two—it increased by a factor of four!

From a RISC standpoint, this was an extremely frustrating and discouraging development. After all, what good did it do to try to increase the speed of a processor by adding more transistors if a greater and greater portion of the processing power you were trying to add got burned up in overhead? Overhead in this case is similar to the kind of overhead you'll find in a manufacturing organization—costs that cannot be avoided, but do not contribute to the bottom line except to soak up funds.

The overhead on a processor actually originates from the transistors whose job it is to take instructions from the compiler that are to be executed. These transistors try to organize and arrange instructions in such a way that the processor can figure out which of these can be executed at the same time (i.e., in parallel). The logic that is required to do this is the real contributor to overhead on a processor, because it demands an ever-larger number of transistors to track and determine how to run these instructions.

The increased overhead when trying to push for higher performance gave us very definitive results. Predictably, the performance curve began to flatten out as we tried to develop the chip beyond the 4-issue architecture. This made developing more powerful parallel processing RISC-based chips an expensive and unattractive option to HP. It all but proves out Moore's Second Law, where the cost of producing more powerful chips became economically unattractive.

Explicit Parallelism

Even before the development of the Intel® Itanium® processor family[19] and its EPIC architecture, the business processes in an enterprise environment were massively parallel, though most computers in use to manage these business processes today are not. Things don't happen in a sequential order—multiple things are happening at the same time throughout the entire day in order for the business to run smoothly.

Were the world to run in a purely sequential manner, output would be reduced to a crawl. Thus, the concept of doing things in parallel at the microprocessor level makes intuitive sense; the challenge is to make this happen "explicitly" rather than the implied parallelism of today's RISC systems where the parallel operations occur on the fly.

Finding Parallelism on the Fly

Past hardware efforts, specifically superscalar RISC with out-of-order execution, focused on finding small bits of parallelism on the fly. As the RISC processor gets instructions from the compiler, it actually has an instruction 'buffer' that tries to determine what it can process in parallel. For example, the buffer's analysis might determine that as the processor executes a set of calculations that are embedded in a given loops, it can also execute the code immediately before it while the calculations run.

But given the fact that the processor has to do this in the middle of fetching and executing instructions, the selections for parallel computing cannot be very large. It requires a fairly high level of complexity to even figure out what limited operations can be done in parallel. Therefore, processors today can actually run in a limited parallel mode—but by and large they are still confined to single instruction threads within software modules.

Multithreading and Finding Better Parallelism Opportunities

Operating system efforts focused on multiple threads and processes. Typically, this is through what is called 'multithreading'. This increases system throughput, but it's ultimately bounded by processor throughput. The processor remains the 'bottleneck' in the system.

By moving to the new EPIC parallel architecture, we're actually able to move the responsibilities for finding the opportunities for parallelism back into a software model. Once the compiler is running, it has to 'see' the entire program. So it gets a

---

19.   Intel and Itanium are registered trademarks or trademarks of Intel Corporation or its subsidiaries in the Unites States and other countries.

very broad look at the information that needs to be processed, and locates many more opportunities to run items in parallel.

The compiler can now identify opportunities for second level parallelism, or even break a program into separate parallel 'blocks'. This achieves a much broader scope, and creates new opportunities to exploit parallelism. This one development alone allows us to move beyond the current limitations of semiconductor technology. Figure 7-2 below provides a graphic illustration of how the compiler would work in this architecture environment.

The Register Model

RISC or CISC machine registers are actually the processor's 'fastest' memory. This memory resides directly on your processor. They're designed to be short-term memory locations that can hold addresses, data, or instructions. The idea is that there is little or no latency when pulling information from the register. Latency simply refers to the delay or lag time when seeking out or returning information.

Registers as Storage Locations

Registers are used for is also a temporary storage location for a value. For example, say that you were going to multiply a table of numbers by a constant. If the constant is placed in the register, every time you fetch one of the numbers in the table, the processor simply pulls the constant from the register quickly and completes the calculation in the quickest amount of time.

IPF architecture: explicit parallelism

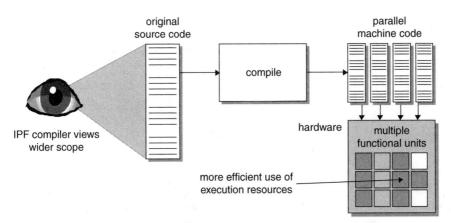

Figure 7-2   Itanium Processor Family Architecture: Explicit Parallelism

Registers Help to Expose the Parallelism

Any microprocessor needs more registers to expose more parallelism in the code. In a typical enterprise-computing environment, where we want to execute multiple instructions at a time and take advantage of parallel operations, there is a need to keep track of "all of the balls in the air". To keep track of these "balls in the air" requires more registers, or at least more register names. More registers enable a wider issue machine (Itanium processors can issue 6 instructions per cycle), and allow a deeper pipeline to get more things done in parallel.

Itanium Processor Register Set Model

The EPIC architecture upon which the Itanium processor is based allows for a large number of registers. The 128 floating-point registers combine both fixed and rotating registers. The rotating registers are normally used for software pipelining loops to greatly speed up loop execution. This allows the encoding of common algorithms without running the risk of depleting the available register space. It also allows you to move data between registers without having to resort to complex tricks that slow the processor down.

The Itanium microprocessor's large register set provides a place to store intermediate results during complex calculations. Latency is reduced, as going back to on-chip cache or the off-chip RAM for a memory read or write would result in a delay due to the extra steps (latency) involved. The Itanium processor registers also act as a buffer to store data between the functional units and the memory, thereby lessening the likelihood of 'stalls' in the software pipeline. These stalls result from the lack of data and also are responsible for slowing down the overall speed of applications. By avoiding this scenario, a higher rate of sustained parallel performance is more easily achieved.

Floating Point Architecture

Floating-point calculations, which involve mathematical computations between numbers with large numbers of decimals, are done on a separate 'floating point' registry. In the Itanium processor's architecture, floating-point operations are performed with these registers as extended precision calculations. Since floating point can take advantage of 64-bits of precision, the Itanium processor has a natural advantage in handling numbers with a large number of decimal places, extreme amounts of precision and can reduce 'round-off' error, as discussed in Chapter 4's section on 'Early Adopters'. The 82-bit register design allows the Itanium processor to extend the calculations out to a much larger number of decimal places, thus providing a higher level of accuracy that is critical in many scientific applications.

The floating-point architecture is a perfect example of the interplay that occurs between a number of EPIC concepts. Software and hardware features blend to make a unique floating-point architecture that has both high performance and excellent accuracy. Floating point performance is key to many applications in scientific computing, life sciences, and areas of business intelligence and e-commerce where more analytical workloads are processed.

Floating-point specific instructions like the Floating Point Multiply Add (FMA) removes intermediate rounding stages, so speeding the execution of some floating-point calculations without increasing the error produced by rounding. This extra accuracy has made Itanium even more valuable in certain functions: rendering applications, simulations, and security areas such as encryption/decryption.

For these reasons, Itanium's EPIC architecture is rightly considered in two ways: the next generation of chip architecture, and also a break from the RISC tradition of processing.

In Summary

- EPIC is the next enterprise computing architecture, not simply an evolution of RISC.
- Under EPIC, the compiler can scan and locate much broader areas to process in parallel, thus allowing for a much larger speed gain.
- The Itanium processor's design allows for much larger registers. Registers act as intermediate storage locations for values to reduce the delay in getting instructions and data from memory locations to the processor to speed up processing.
- Finally, these larger registers provide superior performance and accuracy when performing computations involving large, floating-point numbers.

Key Architectural Changes in EPIC

In a very real sense what we were trying to do was go explicitly for high levels of instruction parallelism that were easily generated by a compiler and to eliminate all this hardware complexity that was growing up around the out-of-order superscalar implementations of RISC machines. And this is really—and this is really what led to EPIC.

—Bill Worley (RISC and EPIC architect)

In This Chapter:

- Memory management in EPIC
- Predication
- Branch prediction tables
- Static and dynamic branching
- Speculation
- Software pipelining

The whole purpose of the Intel Itanium architecture[20] is to use every practical technique to increase parallelism so that the processor can execute as many instructions per cycle as possible and to have the resources to ensure that this rate can be

---

20.   Intel and Itanium are registered trademarks or trademarks of Intel Corporation or its subsidiaries in the United States and other countries.

sustained as best as possible. This can be accomplished because of the design philosophy at the heart of the Itanium processor family—the Explicitly Parallel Instruction Computing (EPIC) philosophy.

EPIC defines why Itanium-based processors are different from other 64-bit processors by enabling much higher levels of instruction level parallelism without unacceptable increases in hardware complexity. EPIC does this by placing the burden of finding that parallelism squarely on the compiler, which can review the entire code stream and make global optimizations.

Memory Management in EPIC

An immediate advantage of Itanium over older processor technologies is the move from 32-bit-based systems (especially if you have IA-32 systems) to systems based on 64 bits. You can address a lot more memory on your machine, which allows you to manage much larger sets of data, and thus handle larger workloads more efficiently and mine data more effectively.

Memory Hierarchy Control

EPIC allows you to exercise much more control over the memory hierarchy. Memory exists in a hierarchical fashion on the machine. The registers are the fastest and closest to the microchip but also the smallest piece of memory. Next in line is what's known as the level 1 cache, which can also exist on the chip. It's fast, though not as fast as registers. The next fastest memory is the level 2 cache. This level can exist on the same chip, though it also may be based on a chip-on-a-chip module.

Further down the line is the level 3 cache, and at the bottom of the hierarchy is the disk drive itself. As you continue down the hierarchy, each level of memory gets bigger, though the access time gets slower. This is a function of the size allocated to the memory level and its degree of remoteness from the chip itself—the farther away it is, the longer the access time.

Built into the EPIC architecture is the ability for the processor to actually give some hints as to which level of cache should be used to store different variables or functions. It can tell the processor which level of memory is going to be needed first. By doing so, the processor can rank what it places in memory on the basis of which instructions it will need loaded first. Where older processors might simply fill up the cache on a sequential basis—fastest first, then the next faster, and so on—EPIC allows each area to sync up with the processor's needs as they arise within the execution of a program.

Predication

Predication refers to the ability to better manage branches in a given program. Predication is a great example of the architecture's ability to do multiple things in parallel. A typical out-of-order execution engine maintains a couple of different program counters at the same time. One keeps track of the program instruction currently being executed, while the other is looking ahead at instructions that will be executed in the future. It builds a *pipeline,* or *queue,* to speed the transaction when it actually occurs. An excellent example of how this works is shown in Figure 8–1.

This whole process makes the chip extremely efficient, since it focuses on the task at hand while at the same time plotting out what it will be handling next. The objective is the have the instructions and data immediately available to the processor(s) so that the high speed computing components never have to wait for anything. Waiting is seen as a 'stall' in the system. But to better understand predication, we have to look at how a typical RISC machine handles branches today in an effort to keep the processor busy.

Branch Prediction Tables

Programs have a lot of different branches, or if–then–else conditions, which change the values fed to the processor depending on which branch is selected. A code decision construct typically involves an if–then–else form, such as

```
if a = b, then
    x = a - b
else
    y = a + b
end
```

predication process illustrated

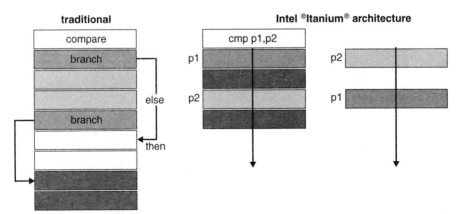

Figure 8-1   Predication Process Illustrated

This translates to assembly code similar to a branch followed by the subtraction or addition and a return from a branch.

In a RISC (and in an EPIC) machine, a *branch prediction table* resides directly on the chip itself. If the table notes that the branch goes to A 78 percent of the time and only 22 percent of the time to B, then it builds the pipeline for that direction of branch A. A visual example of how this works can be seen in Figure 8–2.

There are two forms of branch prediction: static and dynamic. Static branch prediction takes place when the compiler does the compile: it actually gets some information from the code that enables it to determine which branch direction is selected the majority of the time. This information is used to build the initial branch prediction table.

Dynamic branch prediction takes place on the chip in real time. As the chip executes the program, it notes inaccuracies in the static branch table (where the prediction says that 75 percent of the time the result is A when it's actually B). The chip can dynamically update the table to reflect the accurate information and restore the higher level of efficiency needed to run at the best speed. This is especially important given that programs themselves are not static. Depending on the conditions that the program is running under, the normal assumptions of the branch prediction table could be significantly different than the actual needs.

The problem occurs when the branch prediction is wrong, because all of the work that was done by the processor looking ahead and executing instructions beyond the branch is lost. If a pipeline has been built for the choice that is not taken, it is dumped and the program must start executing the new branch—which again wastes time and terminates the advantage of processing items in parallel.

Predication allows the elimination of this type of branch. In the example above, say that both the if and else statements (x = a – b; y = a + b) can be executed

example of predication

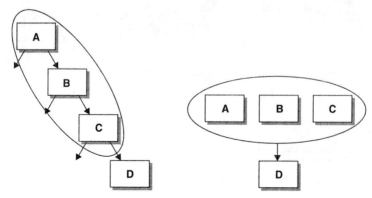

Figure 8-2   Prediction Process Code Sample

in parallel. In that case, the predicate register determines which of the conditional results should be used as the program proceeds to the next step.

The key benefit of predication is that it eliminates branches, thereby reducing the performance penalties associated with mispredicted branches. Predication provides a mechanism for easing into conditional branches wherever possible that would otherwise interrupt instruction-level parallelism.

Branch predication enables the removal of branches by taking both paths of execution and discarding the inaccurate outcome. Predication is an important technique to maximize parallelism, as mispredictions can cause many lost opportunities to issue new instructions. Predication can take on different forms depending on the function that is being performed.

Data Speculation

EPIC also speeds up processing by a technique know as *data speculation*. Speculation works to reduce the memory latency, which is the delay time to access and move data to and from memory. Typically, memory speed is slower than the processor speed, which causes the processor to wait or "stall" for several clock cycles each time it must access memory. As a general rule, today's systems have memory that runs at about half the speed of the processor.

With speculation, the program is able to put all the "load instructions" at the start of a routine. As the loads are processed, other set up or processing can be performed so that when the program is ready to use the load results, the data is ready to use. As an example, see Figure 8–3.

This type of operation can be performed in today's RISC and CISC machines; however, the problem is that the program is "speculating" that the data will still be

example of data speculation

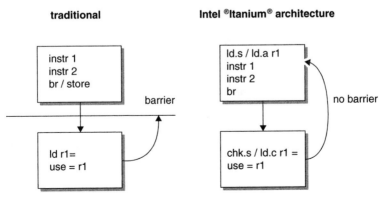

Figure 8-3 Data Speculation

valid when it is used. If it is not, then some error recovery routine is required to reload the data before the program can proceed. Not only does this require more code, but if the programmer fails to include the error recovery, the results could be disastrous.

Load instructions in an Itanium-based computer can be executed with a "check." Much like the predication example, this check option allows a bit to be set if the data that was loaded is good; that is, it has not been modified since the load occurred. If the check is okay, the data is used, and the process continues. If not, the data is reloaded transparently to the program.

One hardware feature that improves efficiency in this area is the advanced load address table (ALAT) that allows loads to be potentially executed before stores. First, a load is executed, and then the special check instruction is executed. The check instruction examines the ALAT to determine if a dependency exists and if the speculative load is indeed correct. Figure 8–4 provides an example of this in action.

Speculation becomes a key component as processor speeds continue to outpace the speed of system memory. Continued work in speculation enables Itanium to reduce or eliminate much of the latency involved during access to system memory because of the disparity between the speeds of the processor and the memory itself.

Software Pipelining

The software pipelining process allows faster execution of loops in a given program. In its simplest form, a program's loop construct is one that repeatedly performs the same operations. This program structure is often found in scientific and

example of speculation in a code block

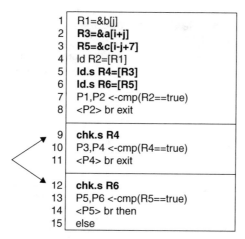

Figure 8-4   Control/Data Speculation Shown in Code Block

technical computing and in heavy mathematical functions, as they tend to process large amounts of data in a similar fashion to isolate patterns or test out the result of a change to long lists of data. However, it is also common in many commercial applications.

Since these loops generally encompass a large portion of a program's execution time, a major speed gain can be made to expose as much loop-level parallelism as possible. With Itanium, a special set of application registers allow the loop to be executed in parallel. These special registers enable features such as managing the loop count, handling the renaming of registers for the pipeline, and finishing work in progress when the loop ends.

A prime example of this can be seen in Figure 8–5, which shows how parallelism can execute multiple instances of the loop at a single time.

In Summary

- EPIC architecture enables the processor to give some hints as to which level of cache should be used to store different variables or functions. By doing so, the processor can rank what it places in memory on the basis of which instructions it will need loaded first.
- Predication allows the virtual elimination of branches and can avoid the problems of misprediction of the branch outcome.
- The branch prediction table resides directly on the chip itself. The table is used to collect real-time information on what the program is doing: It builds statistics on which branch is used and how often.
- Speculation reduces the memory's latency, which is the delay time to access the memory, while software pipelining allows faster execution of loops in a given program.

representation of software pipelining

traditional   Intel ®Itanium® architecture

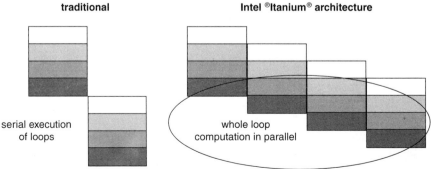

serial execution   whole loop
of loops   computation in parallel

Figure 8-5 Software Pipelining

CHAPTER 9

Total Cost of Ownership Under Itanium

People in information technology today are looking at the cost of transactions as a way of determining TCO...and because of the amazing price–performance of a platform like Itanium, you can measure this. You're actually adding to the bottom line of the company with Itanium. In essence you're using technology to increase your margins, and margins drive profits.

—Kurt Steele, independent consultant for SAP Systems

In this Chapter

- TCO methodology
- ROI predictors
- The four main TCO solutions
- HP's solution framework for TCO management

Today's IT departments have learned the wisdom of weighing the *total* costs and benefits of owning and operating technology. Rather than merely comparing the price of hardware options, they also have begun evaluating the indirect costs of installation, training, upgrades, and other requirements. Total cost of ownership (TCO) is seen as a more holistic view of IT costs across enterprise boundaries; see Figure 9–1.

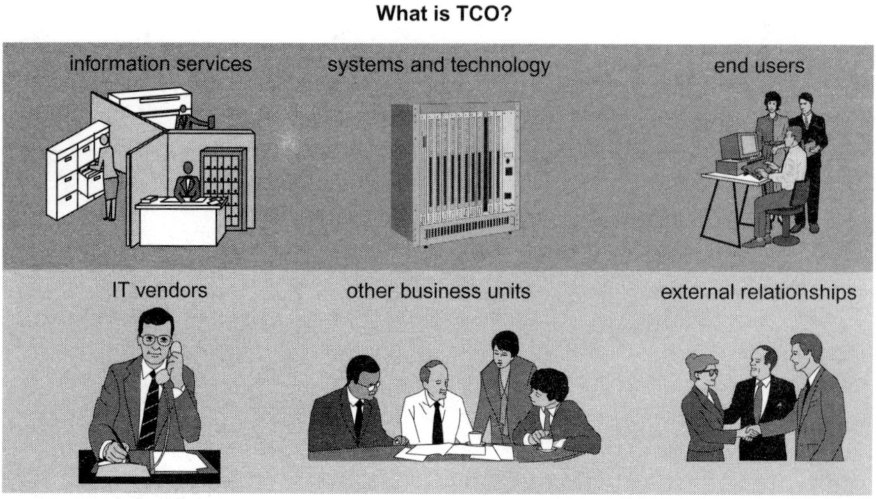

What is TCO?

Figure 9-1   What Is TCO?

TCO Methodology

The tools for measuring TCO have evolved rapidly, particularly for the client side of distributed computing environments. TCO has become a comprehensive set of methodologies, models, and tools to help organizations better in two ways: first, by improving overall value of IT investments, and second, by measuring, managing, and reducing costs. This can be expressed as a continual cycle of improvement, as demonstrated in Figure 9–2.

The TCO is the cost of procuring, deploying, and maintaining management information systems. According to GartnerGroup, "A 10 percent saving in non-purchase costs—something most corporations can easily achieve through the adoption of HP management technologies—is the equivalent of a 50 percent saving in buying price." It is purchase price, however, that often receives most of the attention when savings are sought; but here the market is so competitive that only a small percentage savings can be achieved. The purchase price is not the place to look for real savings.

Perhaps the most telling aspect of the continued integration of high-performance networks and computers today is that some costs continue to fall while other costs rise. As the cost of client/server hardware technology declines, the cost of managing this technology continues to escalate. While life cycle management costs climb, end-user satisfaction and productivity steadily fall. In that sense, many of the

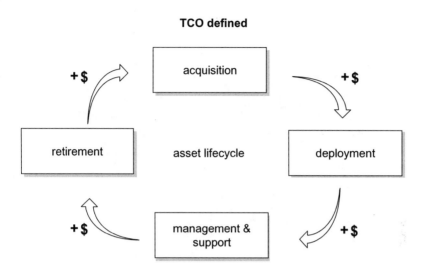

Figure 9-2 TCO Asset Life Cycle

costs of any given system are hidden, similar to the way much of an iceberg's mass is hidden below the waterline, as in Figure 9–3.

The initial purchase of hardware is a small expense in comparison to the dangers lurking "just below the surface." The long-term costs of maintaining and supporting the computing infrastructure of a mission-critical environment include training, support, administration, asset tracking, and upgrades.

The result is that the TCO is of increasing interest to companies that want to better manage their environment. As seen in Figure 9–4, not managing these costs allows them to grow instead of decline.

ROI Predictors

Many of the returns in ROI (return on investment) analysis are intangible or difficult to quantify. For example, it is nearly impossible to assign a dollar value to improved customer service, even though better service undoubtedly helps build customer loyalty and retention. In spite of the difficulties, such returns often reflect the true value of IT investments. They are crucial to a total analysis of technology and should be the focal point of a technology evaluation.

Demand is now growing for a standard method of analyzing the enterprise server side of the client/server model. As the open-services marketplace continues to evolve, the need for an objective evaluation of TCO and ROI for enterprise servers becomes even more critical. Enterprise servers are the engines driving this

TCO: the business justification

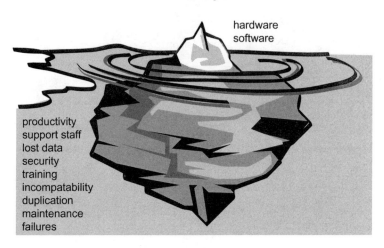

Figure 9-3   Total Cost of Ownership

cost categories explored in TCO analyses

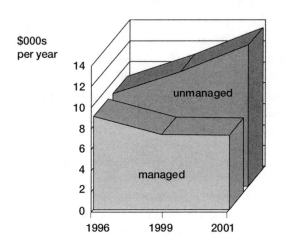

Figure 9-4   Managed versus Unmanaged Costs

computing paradigm. That is why it is more important than ever to select the right technology.

When organizations consider purchasing new technology, they typically want to know how the technology can enhance the strength and health of their business. In other words, they want to evaluate what the return might be on their investment. Tools for analyzing the ROI are continually in development. ROI analysis generally concentrate on three general categories: new business opportunities, investment protection, and a total life cycle framework.

New Business Opportunities

Today, there is a rush of companies implementing e-commerce, e-services, data mining, and other applications. It's obvious that new technology can open up new markets and create new profit centers. The challenge is deciding if the value of the new opportunities justifies the investment.

Even when technology does not enable new business opportunities, new systems can enable businesses to operate more efficiently and effectively. Technology can create a competitive advantage by giving companies an edge in several areas, including:

- Heightened employee productivity through the ability to handle repetitive tasks automatically.
- Faster time-to-market through better communication and collaboration.
- Improved customer satisfaction through improved response times and higher system availability.
- Product and service quality improvements through quality assurance applications and enhanced data analysis.

Investment Protection

When companies have already invested in technology, they want to leverage those previous expenditures. If two proposed systems provide comparable business opportunities and enhanced competitiveness, organizations generally choose the one that can provide the greatest protection of the current investments. This was one of the key goals of the joint Hewlett-Packard–Intel design team and why HP has also put considerable planning into the transition process. This will be described in more detail in the following chapters. You will also learn more about the binary compatibility to protect software investments.

A Total Life Cycle Framework

Incorporating the total life cycle and solution into TCO analysis is still not comprehensive enough. If the user considers just the TCO of various options, he or she could easily waste IT dollars on technology that underperforms or overperforms. TCO can determine which option is least costly, but it cannot tell which option can provide the greatest competitive advantage.

For the most useful analyses, IT consumers must scrutinize both the potential costs and the potential benefits of their systems. In essence, they can combine TCO analysis with ROI analysis. A solid benefits analysis can determine which platforms are viable without expensive, time-consuming cost analyses. Organizations can develop shortlists of systems that meet minimum requirements and then perform cost studies.

The Four Main TCO Solutions

The end goal of any TCO solution is to reduce costs as much as possible to improve the return on the initial investment. To that end, there are four main solutions promulgated by HP:

- Simplification by standardization
- Management solutions
- Business protection
- Life cycle management

Simplification by Standardization

Of course, reducing the heterogeneity of your network of computers (moving away from a mixed network) is the easiest simplification remedy for end-user support. The Intel Itanium[21] processor family helps you with this aspect because the HP and Intel alliance set to design a microprocessor architecture that could become the new industry standard for enterprise servers and high-end workstations. If you can standardize on the architecture at the level of the microprocessor, you can immeasurably simplify the support systems you need to have in place to handle it. It also enhances effective systems management. If you have to manage many systems, it's a lot easier if they are more homogenous.

Systems maintenance also becomes much easier and less costly. More homogenous machinery and few servers (such as Itanium's solution) mean that you'll require fewer replacement parts. Furthermore, the ones you do need will more often than not be common parts, allowing swapping and replacement.

Standardization also reduces training expenditures in both dollars and hours, not only for the end users, but also for the IT departments that support the end users. This in turn reduces the cost of an IT department, which needs to hire fewer people, with a more core set of necessary skills.

Finally, it simplifies technology planning. When you have a single Itanium-based server that can support three operating systems, it's easier to plan how to

---

21.   Intel and Itanium are registered trademarks or trademarks of Intel Corporation or its subsidiaries in the United States and other countries.

grow and maintain your entire data processing resource, because you're only really working with one architecture from the desktop to the data center—the Itanium architecture.

Hewlett-Packard Management Solutions

HP provides a software-based management solution called Openview. Openview is a common set of management tools that provide the services listed in Figure 9–5.

Most importantly, Openview allows you to have a common view across all three major operating systems. Whether you are running Linux[22] Windows,[23] or HP-UX, you have management tools to work in each operating environment.

The benefits of using Openview include:

• Integrated management of Itanium-based, PA-RISC-based, and IA-32-based platforms.
• Ease of use.
• Access through a Web browser provides virtual presence and control anytime and anywhere.
• Industry-leading server management tool since 1991.
• Estimated over 1.5million servers managed.

openview management services

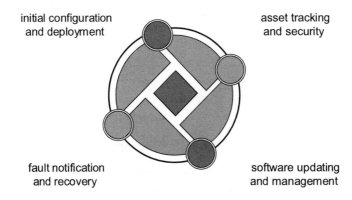

initial configuration and deployment

asset tracking and security

fault notification and recovery

software updating and management

Figure 9-5 Openview Services for Change Management

22.   Linux is a registered trademark of Linus Torvalds.
23.   Windows is a registered trademark of Microsoft Corporation..

- Web-based event management, proactive notification, system software maintenance, and links to lights-out technology.

Best of all, Openview can be up and running in minutes on a desktop or server.

Business Protection

Itanium-based solutions protect your organization from loss of data and reduce the lost productivity associated with downtime. Aside from the lost revenue resulting from missed customer opportunities, this also keeps a major expense under control—the expense that results from tens or hundreds of highly paid information technology, industrial, or financial employees being idle at their desks when a major outage hits.

Life Cycle Management

With effective life cycle management, you can maximize the return on your IT investments. For example, your IT organization may run 30 percent of the company's network on Windows, 10 percent on Linux, and 60 percent on UNIX. Normally, any major shift in these percentages means a tremendous amount of upheaval and expenditure.

Not so with Itanium-based systems and Itanium's ability to support multiple operating environments, where you can simplify service and support management while creating seamless technology transitions. You can switch the operating environment as your needs change and redeploy systems throughout the life cycle of various machines and operating systems without replacing your server multiple times. For example, if all of your applications run on UNIX today, but in the future some new release comes out on Windows or Linux, an Itanium-based server can handle the OS change and allow you to manage the life cycle of your IT assets much more easily. Major capital investments are avoided, as you don't have to throw the hardware out—you simply repurpose it.

HP's Solution Framework for TCO Management

Hewlett-Packard is uniquely positioned to manage TCO by leveraging its experience as the leading provider of client/server services and financing in mixed computing environments. Due to the immense capabilities of the Itanium processor family, HP enterprise servers can deliver competitive TCO and high ROI because various HP programs address costs and benefits at every level of the solution—hardware platforms, operating environments, middleware, ISV solutions, and service and support. See Figure 9–6.

TCO solution framework

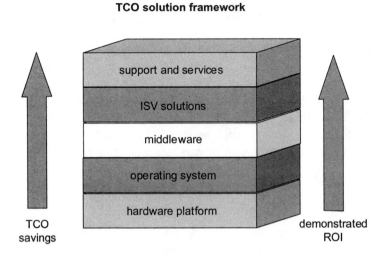

TCO
savings

demonstrated
ROI

Figure 9-6   Solution Framework

Hardware Platform

To protect software investments and further reduce TCO, HP-UX has supported application binary compatibility since 1986. Future HP platforms utilizing Itanium power continue this ideal. For example, legacy 32-bit HP-UX applications run seamlessly on the 64-bit Itanium technology. The same is true for 32-bit Windows and Linux applications running on Itanium-based systems.

Operating Systems

Long committed to true open systems computing, HP believes it is wrong to dictate to customers which operating environment they should choose. That is because Hewlett-Packard understands the reality of today's computing environments—mixed environments are becoming more prevalent as complex market and computing requirements continue to drive technology decisions. Choices such as which operating system to use must be made based on these drivers, and systems should be selected based on where they make the most sense and offer the greatest functionality.

Middleware

HP middleware helps lower costs and bolster ROI through a broad portfolio of high availability (HA) solutions. Servers running Itanium are already proven to have higher uptimes and faster recovery times. Because of this, customers running Itanium-based systems will be far less likely to lose sales or miss transactions.

Applications

Itanium-based enterprise servers will seamlessly support thousands of leading ISV solutions. Customers who choose Itanium-based solutions will have virtually no limit on the software solutions they can use to minimize costs and maximize benefits. The list of new software applications will continue to grow as the family of systems expands and new software vendors recognize the potential of this pervasive architecture.

Services and Support

HP runs a one-stop support network that keeps a customer's support costs to a minimum. From the benefits perspective, HP consulting services help the client design systems that provide a competitive advantage and higher ROI.

In Summary

- The tools for measuring TCO have evolved rapidly into a comprehensive set of methodologies, models, and tools to help organizations in two ways: by improving overall value of IT investments and by measuring, managing, and reducing costs.
- ROI analysis is often intangible or difficult to quantify. In spite of the difficulties, such returns often reflect the true value of IT investments. They are crucial to a total analysis of technology and should be the focal point of a technology evaluation.
- Technology can create a competitive advantage by giving companies an edge in faster time-to-market through better communication and collaboration, improved customer satisfaction through improved response times and higher system availability, and product and service quality improvements.
- The goal of any TCO solution is to reduce costs as much as possible to improve the return on the initial investment. To that end, there are four main solutions promulgated by HP: simplification by standardization, management solutions, business protection, and life cycle management.
- Due to the capabilities of the Intel Itanium processor family, HP enterprise servers can deliver competitive TCO and high ROI because various HP programs address costs and benefits at every level of the solution—hardware platforms, operating environments, middleware, ISV solutions, and service and support.

The Transition Process

"That Itanium...provides a fairly linear improvement path [is due to its] use of massive explicit parallelism. We're still trying to figure out the quantification of that performance jump. And several people have told me that this jump is a multiple—two times faster, three times faster, four times faster.:

—Jerry Huck

In this Chapter:

- Toward transitioning to Itanium
- The five phases of the Itanium transition process
- Planning phase
- Porting and transition
- Implementation support
- Hardware and software
- Education

The Itanium implementation of Explicitly Parallel Instruction Computing (EPIC) technology combines the concepts of explicit parallelism, predication, and speculation to progress well beyond the limitations of traditional architectures. This will enable industry-leading performance far into the future.

Itanium is the first mainstream architecture designed from the beginning to take advantage of parallel execution. With its massive resources, inherent scalability,

IPF capabilities	IPF benefits
support for HP-UX, Windows and Linux	• develop on one system, deploy on multiple operating systems • standardize on a common server, with the flexibility to optimize the environment by using the best operating system for specific situations
IA-32 and PA-RISC backwards compatibility	• make the transition to titanium in stages • thousands of applications can run unchanged on Itanium in compatibility mode
64-bit addressing to work with large amounts of data in memory	• applications that are database-dependent, such as CRM and ERP environments, will run considerably faster than on 32-bit systems
unsurpassed encryption/decryption	• accelerate secure transmissions over the web, such as e-commerce transactions and confidential communications
extremely fast floating point calculations	• improved performance in technical and financial fields for applications, such as protein folding and drug design, computer-aided engineering (CAE) and digital stock trading
ability to support faster multimedia applications	• entertainment software will reach a new level by accelerating digital content creation
inherent scalability	• expandable bandwidth forms the basis for performance improvements in future generations
large number of registers	• exceptional performance for floating-point and integer computations, as well as execution of loop code

Figure 10-1   Itanium Capabilities and Itanium Processor Family Benefits

and full compatibility, the Intel Itanium processor family[24] will be the ideal next-generation processor architecture for high-performance servers and workstations. See Figure 10–1 for a full table list of details.

Navigating the Path to Itanium

Hewlett-Packard created a transition process that makes the move to an Itanium-based platform as seamless as possible. Based on its decades of experience, HP has carefully analyzed customer requirements to create a set of design principles to guide the development of the transition strategy. Upgrade paths for Itanium-based systems are provided that add substantial value through enhanced system performance.

The goal is to provide performance boosts along these recommended paths. HP also continues to protect as much hardware investment as possible when upgrading to Itanium-based systems. As a company, HP's strategy does not require a major application or database upgrade, or a data transition to move to Itanium.

In fact, if PA-RISC is used, no need exists for recompiling the existing application code when transitioning to Itanium. Itanium/HP-UX systems execute PA-

---

24.   Intel and Itanium are registered trademarks or trademarks of Intel Corporation or its subsidiaries in the United States and other countries.

RISC binaries without recompiling. However, to attain the best performance, Itanium-based systems will work best after recompiling IA-32 and PA-RISC applications. Network and system administrators do not have to worry about complex transitions that grow in difficulty with a change in the environment during an upgrade. The HP-UX environment on Itanium will be exactly the same as that on PA-RISC.

There are five components that should be followed in the implementation process:

- Planning Phase
- Porting and Transition Phase
- Implementation Support Phase
- Hardware and Software Support Phase
- Education Support Phase

These can also be thought of graphically, as in Figure 10–2.

Planning Phase

The first step of any transition plan is to determine the best way to leverage Itanium. Immediately after this decision should be a discussion of how to incorporate Itanium into strategic and tactical plans for your own IT department. It is also necessary to plan for new operating systems and application implementations as

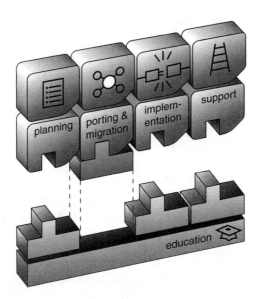

Figure 10-2 The Five Transition Phases of Implementation

well as create a plan to cut over to production mode. Such an assessment should be completed to determine what is required to successfully convert to Itanium.

The assessment should include an evaluation of the general project information, application information, current and future application environments, application sizing, information on required utilities, status of current documentation, data file information, testing requirements, client/server application information, and other miscellaneous items.

The following general project information should be reviewed:

- Determine the objectives of the transition.
- What are the business drivers for the project?
    - Reduced cost of ownership
    - Improved operation efficiency
    - Obsolete platform or environment
    - System consolidation
    - Performance enhancement
- What are the business priorities for the project?
    - Time to market
    - Cost of ownership
    - Scalability
- What is the expectation within IT for the project?
    - Lower cost of ownership
    - Improved performance

In addition, be sure to determine which client operating system is in use: DOS, Microsoft Windows, or UNIX/Linux.[25] Find out if any special or proprietary software is being used in the client environment. Finally, determine the speed and reliability of the client/server communications. From these pieces of information, a cost-benefit analysis can be created. Depending on this analysis result, a detailed strategic and tactical plan can be developed that will drive the actual transition.

Porting and Transition Phase

This phase may not be as important to those who run Itanium in an enterprise environment, because much of the actual porting of the software is likely to have already been done by independent software vendors. However, it's still important to

---

25.   Microsoft and Windows are registered trademarks of Microsoft Corporation.
       Unix is a registered trademark of The Open Group.
       Linux is a registered trademark of Linux Torvalds.

understand the porting and transition options when working through the planning phase to determine what best meets your overall implementation goals.

Unlike with some breakthrough technologies, there is no need to change everything at once when moving to Itanium-based systems. HP provides two methods to migrate applications to the Itanium platform: binary compatibility mode and native binary mode. A major portion of the implementation is selecting which applications should be run in binary compatibility mode and which should be fully ported to native compatibility mode.

Binary Compatibility Mode

Many existing 32-bit and 64-bit applications written for PA-RISC as well as 32-bit applications for Windows and Linux (if 64-bit clean) run immediately on Itanium in binary compatibility mode without recompiling or recoding. This flexibility is a major advantage, especially for corporate developers responsible for large inventories of existing applications.

This level of flexibility requires well-behaved software that uses only public APIs and does not use features that have platform or architectural dependencies. Binary compatibility mode uses a transparent dynamic translator that provides improved performance over current systems, but does not provide the best performance available in the native compatibility mode.

Native Compatibility Mode

While effective performance is available in binary compatibility mode, to achieve the full power of Itanium, it is preferable to run applications in native compatibility mode. This is not an important consideration for nonperformance critical applications, but it is recommended that other applications be ported from binary compatibility mode to native binary mode to take full advantage of the leading-edge Itanium capabilities. This requires recompiling and in a few cases may require some recoding.

Software Transition Toolkit

For 32-bit HP-UX PA-RISC applications, the first step to move to native compatibility mode is to scan for transition impacts. HP has developed a Software Transition Kit (STK) that contains the necessary tools. This will determine the compatibility of the existing applications (if they are well-behaved, use public APIs, and/or use features that have platform or architectural dependencies).

The toolkit will help pick up defect fixes when the shared libraries are patched instead of recompiled, as well as help avoid bindings in architectural dependencies. It is also important to address the 32-bit to 64-bit transition impacts such as data type size differences and potential problems due to data models in the following areas:

- data truncation
- pointers
- data type promotion
- data alignment and sharing
- constants
- bit shifts and bit masks
- bit fields
- enumerated types

The impact of the transition on the networking applications, threads, applications using disk files for information exchange, shared memory usage, compiler differences, and performance implications must be carefully considered. After using the toolkit to analyze the items that need adjustment, the applications can be recoded as necessary to prepare for Itanium implementation. The kit contains the following components:

HP-UX STK Documentation and Tools.   The HP-UX STK contains processes, documentation, and tools that help transition from older to newer HP-UX versions. The STK can help with two types of transition:

- *Source code transition*, when transitioning C, C++, Fortran, or COBOL software and scripts to either the 32-bit or the 64-bit version of HP-UX 11.x on PA systems, or HP-UX 11i version 1.5 on Itanium-based systems.
- *System transition*, when transitioning systems from HP-UX 10.x to HP-UX 11.x on PA systems.

Source Code Transition.   To transition source code, you may have to resolve transition issues such as data model and API changes. Many tools are available to help resolve source code transition issues. API file scanners are provided in the HP-UX STK. Other tools are part of the HP-UX operating system, are included in HP-UX language products, or are supplied by third parties.

System Transition.   The STK also contains instructions that will help you install, upgrade, and configure HP-UX systems. It provides many useful reference documents.

What the HP-UX STK Tools Do

For source code transitions, the HP-UX STK contains two command-line tools to help you identify and fix API transition impacts in HP-UX source files. The tools can also identify opportunities to use some enhanced HP-UX features.

• *Scansummary* helps plan the transition by determining how many and what type of API impacts are in the source files. Certain APIs have changed or are now obsolete—function arguments, results, and behavior may be different.

• *Scandetail* helps perform a transition by indicating exactly what API impacts occur on each line of the source files.

For each impact detected by these tools, a detailed impact page is available that describes the problem and how to resolve it. The impact pages also provide links to background information.

HP-UX Development Solutions

HP has complemented its expertise with targeted acquisitions and partnerships to pull together the most complete, best-of-breed application development ecosystems for Itanium. These development solutions provide the necessary support for specific application transition.

HP-UX Development

HP developed HP-UX 11i v.1.5 for Itanium, so applications written for this platform run on Itanium with complete compatibility for applications and data. HP has created compilers and development tools for C, C++, and Fortran 90 for Itanium, as well as computational libraries.

Thousands of programs will run quite well in Itanium compatibility mode with minimal change, yet these applications run even better after porting to take full advantage of Itanium's distinctive capabilities. Along with the items discussed in this section, HP offers a flexible set of services to help customers through the transition:

• *Porting and Transition Workshop*: A quick investigation of customer's needs followed by development of a high-level strategic plan.

• *Porting and Transition Guidance*: Design services to create a customer's porting and transition strategy.

• *Porting and Transition Detailed Assessment*: An in-depth investigation that yields a detailed transition plan with specific recommendations.

• *Porting and Transition Solution Delivery*: HP works with customers to do the porting and transition of specific applications, including reengineering and integration with existing applications.

• *Online Services*: Customers can tap into HP's expertise online and get assistance with posting and transition questions and challenges.

Implementation Support Phase

Technical support is available for a customer's smooth transition of current applications to an Itanium-based platform. HP's consultants can help you through the steps desired to migrate the applications—from assessment and planning, through porting support, to entire outsourced transition projects. You can specify where you need help.

Since new technologies can be complex, HP has developed the New System Startup Service (an in-depth service designed to bring new Itanium systems up quickly and to familiarize customers with the Itanium technology). The service includes:

• New system startup
• Standard installation
• Basic network configuration
• Configuration of file and accounting structures
• System orientation
• Preliminary evaluation of Itanium customer readiness

Since not every situation requires such a comprehensive approach, HP also offers standard installation services as well as implementation services for secure web solutions.

Hardware and Software Support Phase

Complex computer systems normally have both vendor or manufacturer hardware and software support. With years of knowledge and development, HP is able to support Itanium-based solutions for hardware and software, providing your single point of contact. To extend the value of HP's proactive services during Itanium-platform evaluation, testing, and production planning phases, HP developed PSS: Personalized System Support.

With this service, you are assigned an Account Support Engineer who becomes a continuing partner. This expert stays abreast of developments in your environment and provides ongoing assistance targeted to your specific needs and designed to improve the effectiveness of your IT infrastructure. By doing so, HP is able to combine industry-leading technical assistance with proactive account services.

Education Support Phase

Effective training is crucial for a good transition to an Itanium-based platform. We've tapped the knowledge of the Itanium experts in HP Labs to develop the best training available for this new technology. HP offers an online curriculum that covers overview and administration on all three operating systems: HP-UX, Windows, and Linux. HP can help you bridge the gap between what you know and what you need to know, allowing you to make more informed decisions and move forward quickly. Web-based classes include:

- *Introduction to Itanium*: This training provides an overview of the Itanium architecture, its technical innovations, and how those innovations address today's computing challenges. A case study, numerous examples, and high-level explanations ensure that both technical and nontechnical students can appreciate the strategic relevance of this important new platform in today's marketplace. An overview of this process can also be seen in Figure 10–3.

- *New Features and Functions of HP-UX for Itanium*: This training presentation provides an overview of the changes in the HP-UX operating system for the Itanium architecture (the new EFIand boot process, the Veritas volume manager, and changes in HP-UX/Itanium kernel configuration and logging).

- *Linux on Itanium*: This training presentation provides an overview of the design goals for 64-bit Linux on the Itanium platform together with changes from the IA-32 version. Major Linux distributions and Itanium project members are listed.

- *Windows on Itanium*: This training presentation provides an overview of the design goals for 64-bit Windows on the Itanium platform together with changes from the IA-32 version. Major Windows distributions and Itanium project members are listed.

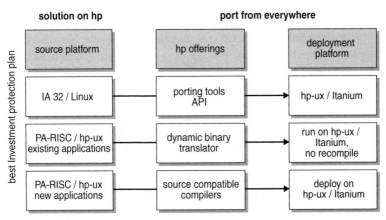

Figure 10-3 How Hewlett-Packard offers porting aides via Linux API support and the Linux Porting Toolkit

- *Migrating Applications to Itanium I*: This training is the first of two presentations that provide an introduction to the transition of applications to the Itanium architecture. A case study and overview of both the development environment and available tools allow students to make an informed decision about transition strategy.
- *Migrating Applications to Itanium II*: This training is the second of two presentations that provide an introduction to the transition of applications to the Itanium architecture. A case study and overview of both the development environment and available tools allow students to make an informed decision about transition strategy.
- *Software Functions and Algorithms on Itanium*: This training presentation provides an overview of the low-level elementary functions and algorithms for the Itanium architecture, in particular floating point.

Conclusions Resulting from the Transition Process

HP customers can expect an easy transition to an Itanium-based platform. Hardware investments are protected through simple system upgrades or, whenever possible, processor board upgrades. PA-RISC application investments are protected as well. Current PA-RISC code running on HP-UX 11.x will run on Itanium-based systems without change.

An incremental approach for moving to Itanium is supported by HP. PA-RISC and Itanium applications can coexist, so there is no requirement of transitioning the entire environment at once. The move can be made when it makes most business sense.

Itanium systems interoperate transparently on existing networks. No changes are required in any of the network services. Minimum user training is required, since the HP-UX environment on PA-RISC and Itanium has the same look and feel. Maximum flexibility is built into HP's Itanium systems as well, allowing the choice of operating environments and tight integration between them.

As a rule, transition to an Itanium system is straightforward and obtainable. The outcome will provide your organization the improved performance necessary to keep up with current application requirements. Whether the transition to Itanium is simple and quick or requires application redesign, HP also offers service capabilities as required. From assessment and design to verification and deployment, HP has the ability to help make transitions seamless.

Finally, HP provides the soundest set of capabilities for transitioning HP system users to the next-generation Itanium environment. HP co-developed the Itanium Instruction Set Architecture with Intel, based on EPIC concepts, and therefore has a head start over other suppliers of this architecture. In addition, the leading application and database vendors are optimizing their software for HP-UX on Itanium.

HP's complete set of consulting, planning, and readiness services is in place to ensure a simple and effective transition to Itanium-based systems.

In Summary

- Hewlett-Packard created a transition process that makes the move to Itanium as seamless as possible. To expedite this, HP proposes a five-step transition plan.
- Planning out the end goal of the Itanium migration will allow you to make the transition in a more fluid manner.
- HP provides two methods to migrate applications to the Itanium platform: binary compatibility mode and native compatibility mode.
- Technical support is available for a customer's smooth transition of current applications to Itanium.
- In addition, HP provides support for hardware, software, and even educational support services.
- Current PA-RISC code running on HP-UX 11.x will run on Itanium-based systems without change. Also, legacy hardware systems are protected. This means that as a rule, HP PA-RISC customers will find it easy to switch to an Itanium-based platform.

The Itanium/HP-UX Transition

"What we intended from the beginning was [that] people who were running UNIX on PA-RISC...would be able to transition to the new [Itanium] architecture relatively easily. It was a core value proposition for us."

—Lew Platt

In This Chapter

- The HP-UX operating system and PA-RISC architecture
- Limitations of RISC leading to Itanium
- HP-UX client investment protection
- Binary compatibility
- Source code compatibility
- HP-UX 11i on the Itanium architecture

Generational transitions that dramatically alter the computing landscape have become more frequent in the past two decades, and the stakes have grown commensurately higher during each shift. In fact, today the transitional risk to enterprises has increased dramatically as computer systems, applications, and data have become an essential part of doing business and speeding up commerce. Because of this, it is important for those who make purchasing and strategic decision in enterprise computing environments to be aware of the ever-escalating life cycle of computing architectures.

Hewlett-Packard began formulating a transition plan in the mid-1990s for HP-UX customers and partners into the next generation of computing architecture. Since these computing architectures were in many ways invented by HP, it made a certain amount of sense to begin thinking in a more proactive manner on these issues. This also provided the basis of the next-generation architecture and the strategy of Hewlett-Packard regarding the newest computing paradigm shift—the transition to the EPIC architecture.

The HP-UX Operating System and PA-RISC Architecture

HP-UX 11i is the latest version of the Unix[26]-based operating system released by Hewlett-Packard. It's an industrial-strength operating system that is well regarded for keeping its UNIX roots in its high level of robustness and extending the basic System V capabilities.

HP-UX 11i is based on the prior incarnation of HP-UX, version 11.00. This earlier version began shipping in late 1997 and was significant in two ways: HP-UX 11.00 was the first version of a UNIX-based operating system that featured a full 64-bit kernel. Also, it was amazingly flexible, able to execute both 32-bit and 64-bit applications in tandem. This 64-bit capability is fortuitous, as the Intel Itanium[27] processor is the first 64-bit next-generation microprocessor released by the alliance of Intel and HP. This is reflected in Figure 11-1.

Version 11.00's concession was that it was available in a 32-bit kernel version as well for older PA-RISC systems that were not 64-bit capable. However, with the

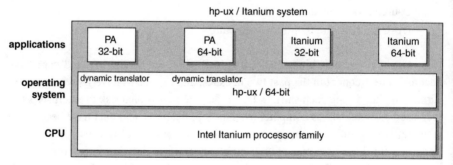

Figure 11-1   IA-64/HP-UX Environment

---

26.   UNIX is a registered trademark of the Open Group.
27.   Intel and Itanium are registered trademarks or trademarks of Intel Corporation or its subsidiaries in the United States and other countries.

64-bit capability, HP-UX 11.00 rose to true enterprise operating system status. The performance, scalability, manageability, availability, connectivity, security, and application availability made it the first choice of many Fortune 1000 companies that run enterprise computing services.

The operating system was in turn enhanced to scale with multiple processors, to support hundreds of gigabytes of main memory, and to support multi-terabyte file systems. With HP-UX 11.00 in place at many sites, Veritas file systems became the standard shipped with all HP-UX systems. Also available was a suite of high-availability products that supported the automatic transfer of applications and users from a failed system to a backup system.

HP-UX system management products enhanced the productivity of system administrators, provided the management of multiple systems from a single console, and supported the distribution of operating system and application software automatically over a network. The most recent improvement in the operating system, HP-UX 11i, is an enhanced version of HP-UX 11.00, which began shipping in December 2000. This new version arrived with two new qualities that made it a standout operating system to work with the new Itanium processor and its brand new EPIC architecture.

1. It retained binary compatibility with the older version, HP-UX 11.00. Existing applications could be moved from HP-UX 11.00 to HP-UX 11i without modification and without recompilation or relinking.
2. HP-UX 11i provided support for the high-end Superdome system. Superdome, with up to 16 hard partitions, support for up to 64 processors, and support for up to 256 gigabytes of main memory, is a giant leap forward for high-end UNIX servers.

Additionally, HP-UX 11i has proven to be a mature 64-bit operating system with excellent quality, reliability, and functionality. HP-UX 11i has achieved higher quality levels than any other release of HP-UX.

Limitations of RISC Leading to Itanium

Architectures based on PA-RISC benefited from the higher clock speeds available on the microprocessors in the 1990s. They also began to take advantage of having multiple functional units on a single machine. The advantage is that it became possible to execute multiple instructions simultaneously and in parallel.

Superscalar RISC processors—RISC processors with the ability to execute multiple instructions simultaneously—began to arrive in the early 1990's. Part of the implementation of these processors was to include logic that examined the incoming stream of instructions for parallel-processing opportunities. Although this examination took up some system resources, the ability to complete two or more instructions on a single clock cycle meant a substantial speed gain could theoretically be achieved without a more expensive chip.

However, to be able to execute multiple instructions simultaneously, RISC processors had to be able to efficiently find parallel-execution opportunities. It turned out that analyzing a stream of instructions and locating parallel-processing opportunities with a high probability of being valid turned out to be a hugely complicated task. The end result was that the branching possibilities of these applications had become too complex for the processor to find parallel-processing opportunities.

This was a serious stumbling block to the increasing performance needs. It became a wall that PA-RISC hit, with no apparent way to breach it. By 1995, RISC architectures were frequently using less than half of the processing power that was available to them. A new processor needed to be designed with the ability to efficiently execute multiple instructions.

To solve this problem, HP Labs developed a concept of parallel processing that evolved into the project known as EPIC, Explicitly Parallel Instruction Computing, which is discussed in detail in chapters 7 and 8. The first Itanium processors based on the EPIC architecture and systems debuted in May 2001. However, Itanium processors are manufactured using the same fabrication facilities as IA-32 processors and therefore benefit from the same manufacturing economies of scale, thus bringing the increased performance level at a previously unheard of price point.

HP-UX Customer Investment Protection

A key component of HP-UX 11i's successful introduction was that Hewlett-Packard offered binary compatibility for all native application software. Cost analysis over the 1990's showed unequivocally that investment in software now far outstrips that of hardware. Therefore, it is more important to provide legacy protection for software than for hardware.

In its design of the Itanium architecture, HP was able to provide a great deal of compatibility with PA-RISC without compromising the performance potential of Itanium. A great deal of compatibility between the PA-RISC and the Itanium architecture was retained. Key aspects of the compatibility between PA-RISC and the Itanium architectures include the following:

- One-to-one mapping of performance-sensitive machine-level instructions between PA-RISC and Itanium architectures.
- Use of the PA-RISC virtual memory architecture for Itanium-based systems.
- Identical data formats between PA-RISC and Itanium architecture.

- Itanium floating-point instructions are a superset of PA-RISC floating-point instructions.
- Itanium multimedia instructions are a superset of the PA-RISC multimedia instructions.
- Itanium graphics acceleration is the same as PA-RISC graphics acceleration.

In addition, HP provides two major types of compatibility between the PA-RISC and Itanium architectures:

1. Binary compatibility (PA-RISC binaries execute transparently on Itanium).
2. Source code compatibility (PA-RISC applications can be converted to native Itanium operation with a recompile; no source code changes are required).

Binary Compatibility

The similarities between the PA-RISC and Itanium architectures allowed HP to develop technology that permits PA-RISC binary executables to execute on the Itanium architecture without modification, recompilation, or relinking. In 1997, HP started work on new dynamic code translation technology. This technology's basis is demonstrated in Figure 11–2.

This technology became known as the Aries project, which we explore further in Chapter 12. The goal of the Aries project was to allow the execution of PA-RISC binaries automatically and transparently on Itanium systems. It is now built into and an integrated component of every version of HP-UX on Itanium, providing the best all-around protection for an organization's legacy software.

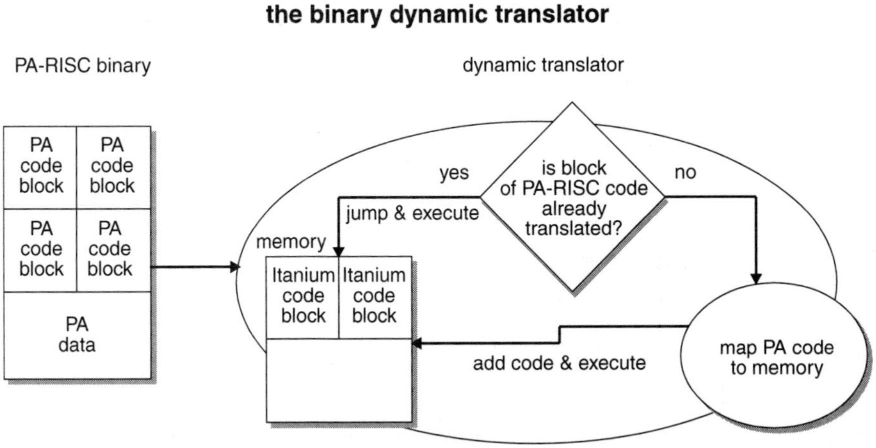

the binary dynamic translator

Figure 11-2   The Binary Dynamic Translator

In addition, this is a boon to clients who are unable to recompile their applications to execute natively on the new architecture. Normally, where binary compatibility is not available, additional methods of transition are available where the source code can be recompiled, as shown in Figure 11–3.

This could be because the application was purchased from a software vendor that has gone out of business and the source code has been lost. Alternatively, the application could be homegrown but the source code has been lost, no longer matches the executable version, or the expertise to maintain the application has been lost. In that case, having built-in binary compatibility is the only available solution to keep a system up and running when moving to a new microprocessor's architecture.

Source Code Compatibility

Source code compatibility between the PA-RISC and Itanium architectures is obtained with HP's compiler technology that divides each compiler into two components:

1. A front-end component that reads the source code and emits metacode.
2. A back-end component that reads the metacode emitted by the front-end component and generates performance-optimized binary code for the specific architecture.

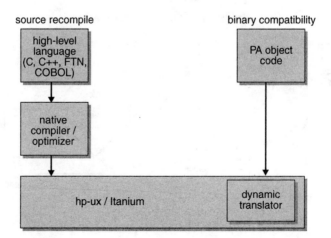

transition methods

Figure 11-3 Transition Methods

The HP compiler structure begins with a language-dependent front end that includes components for lexical analysis, plus syntax and semantic analysis of the incoming source code. Each front end produces an intermediate, stack-based representation of the program for further use by the compiler code generator and optimizers.

Using the strategy of front-end and back-end compiler components, HP is able to use a common front end that provides source code compatibility and different back-end components that generate binary code optimized for either the PA-RISC or Itanium architectures.

HP-UX 11i on the Itanium Architecture

In December 2000, HP-UX work done for Itanium was merged with the HP-UX 11i code stream. This ensured that HP-UX 11i for Itanium-based systems would have the same look, feel, and robust performance as did HP-UX 11i for PA-RISC systems.

HP-UX 11i for Itanium was crafted from the same source code that makes up HP-UX 11i on PA-RISC. Therefore, HP-UX 11i on Itanium-based systems benefits completely from the years of investment that Hewlett-Packard made in HP-UX 11i on PA-RISC. This version of HP-UX defines the standard for an industrial-strength enterprise operating system for mission-critical business applications in these critical areas:

- Performance and scalability: HP-UX 11i is specifically designed and engineered for performance scalability, as evidenced by benchmark results that demonstrate its ability to scale very well for up to 64 CPUs.

- Manageability: HP-UX 11i contains a suite of management tools that can handle servers from both local and remote locations. HP-UX 11i system management tools and products provide extensive capabilities for allocating system resources among application loads.

- Availability: HP-UX 11i incorporates many standard features for excellent single-system availability, such as online component replacement and automatic deallocation of at-risk components.

- Security: HP-UX 11i detects and protects against the most commonly exploited UNIX security vulnerabilities. For example, it is the only operating system to feature its own intrusion detection system.

- Application development: HP-UX 11i supports application development on HP-UX 11i and on Linux and Windows. Application developers can develop and debug their applications on Linux or Windows and then easily deploy on HP-UX 11i.

HP-UX 11i Performance and Scalability

One of the hallmarks of the UNIX-based HP-UX 11i is the ability to maintain high performance levels, even when scaled up to a huge enterprise environment. HP-UX 11i performance scalability derives from several attributes of the basic operating system, including the ability to efficiently support processors of different performance levels and high levels of multiprocessing. It also supports a large range of memory sizes, from megabytes to hundreds of gigabytes, and a file system size of up to 2 terabytes.

These attributes allow HP-UX 11i to function effectively and efficiently on systems ranging from workstations and low-end servers up to very high-end servers. Benchmark results show that HP-UX 11i scales very efficiently for up to 64 processors. Additionally, HP-UX 11i is designed for future scaling up to 256 processors in a single system, and work continues to ensure that potential performance hotspots in the operating system are eliminated. Figure 11–4 shows the scalability of HP-UX 11i with the Broadvision e-commerce application compared to some other leading systems.

HP-UX 11i Manageability

Operating system management capabilities have evolved into a powerful set of tools for HP-UX 11i system administrators. Traditionally, HP-UX system management is built with GUIs for intuitive execution of system management tasks, Web browser access to system consoles (Central Web Console, Secure Web Console), and the ability to failover system management functions to a backup system.

In its latest incarnation, HP-UX 11i system management functions and products are integrated under Servicecontrol Manager. Servicecontrol Manager provides

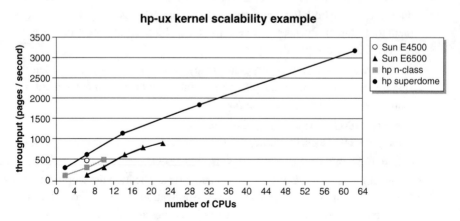

Figure 11-4   HP-UX Kernel Scalability

a single GUI-based interface to all HP-UX system management functions and products. This allows an administrator to manage multiple aspects of the system, including kernel configuration, dynamic allocation of system resources based on service-level objectives, and checking on the currency of security patches.

HP-UX 11i Availability

HP-UX 11i has been recognized for many years as a leader in systems high in availability. HP provides a range of solutions that address varying levels of disaster protection requirements:

- HP Campus Clusters: Campus Cluster solutions create high availability (HA) enterprise clusters with HP 9000 Enterprise Servers up to 10 kilometers apart, offering data and service interruption protection caused by fires and other disasters at a data center.
- HP MetroCluster: MetroCluster reduces business downtime to minutes in the event of system failures or such disasters as fires, grid power outages, and localized floods. Each MetroCluster solution creates a single highly manageable HA cluster with up to 16 HP 9000 Enterprise Servers located as far as 40 kilometers apart, integrating MC/ServiceGuard cluster technology with HP Continuous Access XP or EMC's Symmetrix Remote Data Facility (SRDF)—online, host-independent, data replication solutions.
- HP ContinentalClusters: ContinentalClusters solutions offer fast, simple data recovery between two data centers located anywhere on the planet—offering protection against data loss even during the most severe catastrophes, including earthquakes, floods, and tornadoes.
- The Veritas Journaled File System (JFS): This is included standard with every copy of HP-UX 11i. The Veritas JFS provides efficient, full journaling capability that protects the integrity of both files and the file system. This differs from other journaling implementations that guarantee the consistency of the file system but make no effort to protect the consistency of the files themselves. The full journaling of the Veritas JFS uses transaction logging to ensure the consistency of the files and the file system.
- Autoport Aggregation: HP-UX 11i offers an add-on capability known as Autoport Aggregation allows multiple networking links to appear as one networking link, thus increasing capacity and providing redundancy. If one of the links fails in a group of links that have been Autoport-aggregated, the load automatically and transparently switches to the remaining good links.

HP-UX 11i Security

Hewlett-Packard offers its own host intrusion detection product. This is the Intrusion Detection System/9000 (IDS/9000), which is a major standard feature of HP-UX 11i security capabilities. IDS/9000 enhances local host-level security by near real-time automatic monitoring of each configured host for signs of unwanted and potentially damaging intrusions.

IDS/9000 concentrates on detecting and alarming the HP-UX 11i operating environment at the kernel audit data level of the operating system. It looks for patterns of suspicious activities that suggest security breaches or misuses are underway. When it detects a potential intrusion, it immediately alerts systems management and creates audit events. The alert also has the ability to execute any HP-UX command or program so that a response can be triggered immediately without waiting for human intervention.

Of interest to developers is the Generic Security Services Application Programming Interface (GSS API) for HP-UX 11i. It contains all the GSS APIs in RFC 2743 and is implemented as C programming language interfaces as defined in RFC 2744. Because of GSS API-independence, an application developer writing secure applications needs only to write the code once and does not need to change it whenever the underlying security mechanism changes.

In addition, HP-UX Kerberos provides a Generic Security Services - Application Programming Interface (GSS API). The GSS API provides a standard programming interface that is authentication-mechanism-independent. This allows application developers the flexibility of using alternative authentication technologies, including Kerberos.

HP-UX Application Development

HP recognizes that application and software development platform needs are different from platform needs for the deployment of mission-critical applications. Application and software developers need powerful and flexible integrated development environments (IDEs) running on low-cost platforms.

Mission-critical business applications demand platforms that have wide-ranging performance scalability, high availability, highly productive system management, and bulletproof security. Accordingly, HP has worked with top-tier application development tool providers to construct a set of application development software stacks to fit virtually any application development need.

In Summary

- HP-UX 11i is the latest version of the UNIX-based operating system released by Hewlett-Packard. It's an industrial-strength operating system that is well regarded for keeping its UNIX roots in its high level of robustness and extending the basic System V capabilities.
- HP-UX 11i is based on the prior incarnation of HP-UX, version 11.00. This earlier version began shipping in late 1997. HP-UX 11.00 was the first version of a UNIX-based operating system that featured a full 64-bit kernel.
- Architectures based on PA-RISC benefited from the higher clock speeds available on the microprocessors in the 1990's. However, the end result was that the branching possibilities of these applications had become too complex for the processor to find parallel-processing opportunities. To solve this problem, HP Labs developed a concept of parallel processing that evolved into EPIC.
- HP-UX 11i was crafted from the same source code that makes up HP-UX 11i on PA-RISC. Therefore, Itanium-based systems benefit completely from the years of investment that Hewlett-Packard made in HP-UX 11i on PA-RISC.
- The areas in which HP-UX is optimized for Itanium transition are performance and scalability, manageability, availability, security, and application development.

The Aries Dynamic Code Translation Project

"HP customers who are using PA-RISC systems today will consider purchasing Itanium systems in the future. A number of these customers will consider running their PA-RISC application binaries under the Aries dynamic code translation on Itanium, either for the short term or for the foreseeable future."

—Jon Davis, HP-UX 11 Product Manager

In This Chapter:

- The need for Aries
- Binary compatibility
- The importance of binary compatibility for the IT manager
- The Aries dynamic code translation project
- Aries reliability, usability, and performance
- Results of Aries testing

Normally, the transition to a new architecture requires a tremendous amount of effort and tolerance for systemwide disruption. Fortunately, built into the latest version of HP-UX 11i, which runs on all Itanium-based hardware, is the Aries dynamic code translation technology. This built-in facility transparently executes PA-RISC binaries.

This capability was one of the major goals in the HP–Intel alliance that jointly created the new Intel Itanium processor family architecture.[28] Long-term Hewlett-Packard customers who have enjoyed the performance and price–performance combination of PA-RISC architecture and the HP-UX operating system will not have to make an immediate jump to update all of their current applications. The Intel Itanium processor family, which will dominate the enterprise computing landscape for the next 20 years, was designed with the goal to minimize this disruption to the point that existing users won't have a major headache on their hands when it comes time to make the transition to Itanium power.

The Need for Aries

When we set the project milestones for the Tahoe project with Intel in 1994, one of our shared goals became readily apparent: to protect the software investments of customers and partners on the HP PA-RISC architecture as well as the Intel IA-32 systems. This was to help existing users move their legacy environments and applications—the native applications that they were currently running—into the new Itanium world with a minimum of disruption. A major component in the plan for minimizing this disruption was the Aries project, whose process is illustrated in Figure 12–1.

The goal to provide binary compatibility affected the design of the instruction set for the Intel Itanium architecture. The instruction set of Itanium, although clearly

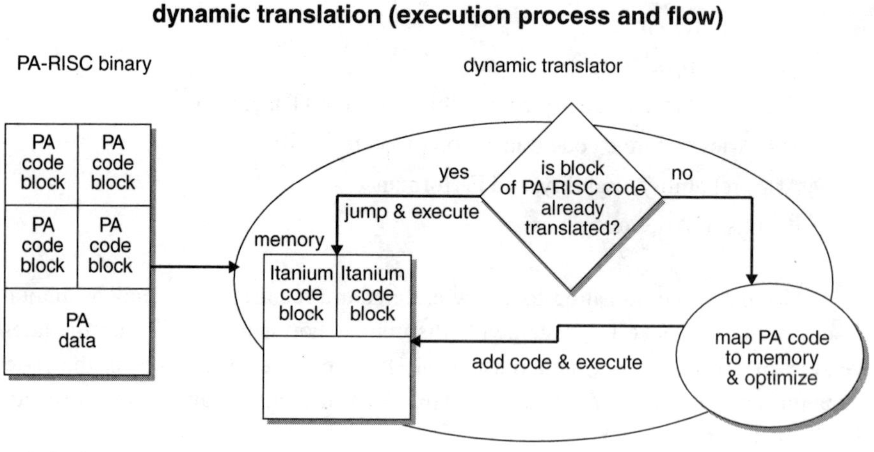

dynamic translation (execution process and flow)

Figure 12-1   The Aries process cycle

---

28.   Intel and Itanium are registered trademarks or trademarks of Intel Corporation or its subsidiaries in the United States and other countries.

designed for the explicitly parallel operation that is the hallmark of the Itanium architecture, was also influenced by the desire to enable a relatively clean mapping between the PA-RISC instruction set and the Itanium instruction set. This mapping led the way for the clean execution of PA-RISC binary code on Itanium.

Binary Compatibility

Binary compatibility says that you can take the program you have today and load the disk onto the new system and it will run. For people in the PC world, this has been a capability that has existed literally since PCs came out. In the early days of PCs, we would test out the level of binary compatibility that existed by running a flight simulator program on the new machine. (Though it sounds a little frivolous, this application was a pretty good test of whether or not the new system would run existing programs.)

Without binary compatibility, the older applications need to be recompiled in order to work on the new machine. A new binary (the code that actually executes when the machine runs) must be created. Aries provides for a customer who has been running HP-UX on a PA-RISC system the needed binary compatibility even though the hardware and the processor underneath has changed significantly.

Aries is a dynamic object code translator. It picks up the binary (which is also known as object code) and translates it from one microprocessor (PA-RISC) to another (Itanium). Therefore, it allows you to run your existing HP-UX software without the need to recompile it.

HP evaluated several different methods of executing PA-RISC binary modules on the Itanium architecture. The approach that HP chose, that of dynamic code translation, offered a number of customer benefits:

1. Dynamic code translation is transparent to the user. No effort on the part of the user is required.
2. Dynamic code translation can be tuned for best performance on specific Itanium processors.
3. The source PA-RISC binary code does not need to be modified as part of the translation process, thus preserving the original binary code.

The Importance of Binary Compatibility for the IT Manager

If you're the manager of a data center, you may have hundreds (or even thousands) of applications to manage on many different platforms. Your customers want constant availability to these applications—and they don't want to see any bumps when the data center changes platforms.

An important consideration is your application mix. First, there are generally a large number of utility applications, such as data formatting and display, and many of these are homegrown—that is, built inhouse. This type of application makes up a large percentage of the overall number of applications. The characteristics of these applications are such that you just want them to run—you don't need them optimized, you don't even want to spend any time converting them, as they aren't enterprise-critical, nor will they be improved much by running at Itanium speeds.

These are the applications that take advantage of binary compatibility. Performance is not the issue here; a guarantee that they'll run in the new environment is. And note that utilities account for the largest number of applications (in terms of quantity), and therefore would be the most costly to convert.

The second type of application are those that are important to the functioning of your business but not a core process. These need to be up and running swiftly but can be optimized later. The key is to get them running quickly and with guaranteed same-as-before correct answers. For most customers, these applications make up 5 percent to 10 percent of the number of applications that they support.

The third type of application are those that go to the core of the business. In general, these are third-party vendor applications, but they can also be inhouse. Typically, there are relatively few of these applications, but they may be the most critical to the core of the business. Therefore, they have to run as fast as possible—giving you the best price–performance and highest absolute performance. These are the prime candidates for optimization under Itanium.

The key is that with binary compatibility, an independent software vendor (ISV) will have an easier time converting the existing HP-UX applications onto an HP platform running HP-UX than onto other vendors' systems. And if the software were being used from a vendor that did *not* have binary compatibility, all of the software products in question would have to be converted.

The conclusion is that binary compatibility has the capability to save you a great deal of capital and minimize disruption for an enterprise that is planning to move to Itanium.

The Aries Dynamic Code Translation Project

Hewlett-Packard has spent years developing and testing the dynamic code translation technology. In fact, the process was considered so valuable that the Aries dynamic code translation project is protected by a number of software patents. The general architecture of the project became encapsulated, as shown in Figure 12–2.

The project began with three main challenges to overcome if binary compatibility was going to lead to seamless client transitions:

1. Reliability: Aries needed to provide hardware-level reliability.
2. Usability: It must be fully transparent—that is, completely unnoticed by the user.

Aries architecture

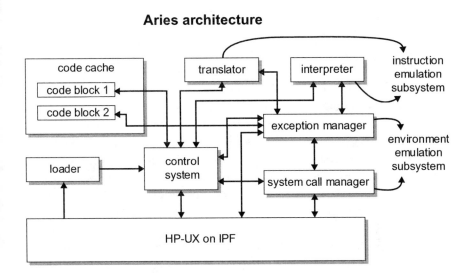

Figure 12-2   Aries Architecture

3. Performance: Performance must be similar in speed to running under the prior architecture.

Aries Reliability

Given the nature of today's IT world —moving ever closer to total integration within a business or scientific endeavor—reliability is a paramount concern. In part this is because many companies are so dependent on their IT infrastructure that they have few options if their applications stop working. In a way, this is similar to what users have come to expect from their hardware—that except for the rare glitch, the system should always be up and running. In that sense, Aries could be considered a kind of virtual microprocessor. It is a software-based solution, but hardware microprocessor verification technologies were used in testing Aries to its limits.

Aries Usability

The vision of the usability aspect was not only to eliminate the need for user interaction, but also to limit or remove developer or system administrator interaction. Installation would not be needed, additional disk space would not be needed—Aries would be completely system transparent, almost a ghost on the machine.

Since Aries is built into the current versions of HP's flavor of UNIX (HP-UX), the operating system automatically detects PA-RISC applications. Once applications are detected, Aries directs them to run under the control of the Aries system. Again, this is done with complete transparency.

Aries Performance

Perhaps the largest issue surrounding the execution of non-native code is performance. In some cases, the execution of non-native code can lead to unacceptable performance degradation. Performance under Aries depends on application characteristics.

HP has performed benchmarks comparing the performance of applications running native on PA-RISC to that of the same applications running under Aries on Itanium-based systems of comparable performance. The objective was to determine the amount of performance degradation that occurred when the application was moved from PA-RISC to Itanium and executed using the Aries dynamic code translation technology.

The results have shown that general commercial applications spending significant time utilizing operating system services and/or performing a large amount of I/O (with mass storage and/or in interaction with users) suffer very little or no performance degradation when using Aries compared to the performance of a similar class PA-RISC system. These applications can be classified as system-intensive applications.

Aries has been optimized to deliver the best performance for commercial applications with the characteristics listed above. Performance for applications that are compute-intensive is more degraded (and applications that are floating-point computation-intensive will see significant performance degradation). Examples of these are technical and analytical workloads or commercial workloads utilizing databases. For these types of applications, recompilation using a native mode compiler is recommended. With very few exceptions, PA-RISC applications can be recompiled for native Itanium mode without modifying source code. For example, 32-bit PA-RISC applications do not need to be converted into 64-bit applications in order to successfully compile on Itanium.

It is also possible to have some executables of an application run under Aries and have other executables run in native mode. A comparison of performance under either architecture is displayed in Figure 12–3.

System-intensive and nonperformance-sensitive applications can run under Aries while performance-sensitive applications can be recompiled for native execution in order to get maximum performance.

Note: Executables on Itanium must be all PA-RISC or all Itanium; mixed-mode executables are not allowed.

Aries application performance comparisons

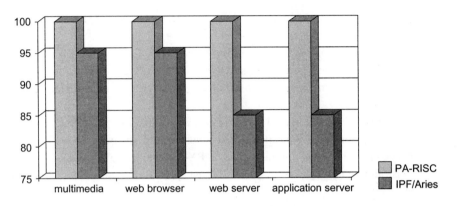

Applications tested included: Netscape, SAM, Apache, Zeus, Xemacs

Figure 12-3   Performance of applications under Aries

Results of Aries Testing

Extensive validation testing was performed on random code sequences using both PA-RISC and Itanium architectures and comparing the results.

The results were unequivocal: Aries was a successful design for a transition aid where it is not possible or desirable (for budgetary or resource reasons) to create a native Itanium binary. Aries allowed existing PA binaries to run on Itanium processors without recompilation. It was completely transparent to the user: automatically invoked by HP-UX, and able to support applications from versions of the operating system 11.0 to 11i. No user effort was required to use Aries.

In addition, it also supported most HP-UX 10.20 applications and both 32-bit and 64-bit applications. Its operation is automatic and transparent whenever a PA-RISC binary is executed. And for many system-intensive applications, it will deliver performance that is near to or equivalent to performance on comparable PA-RISC systems.

In Summary

• Aries was created to help existing customers move their legacy environments and applications—the native applications that they were currently running—into the new Itanium world with a minimum of disruption.

- The Aries project began with three main challenges to overcome if binary compatibility was going to lead to seamless client transitions: reliability, usability, and performance.
- Aries could be considered a kind of virtual microprocessor. The benchmarking and testing of the system was robust.
- Since Aries is built into the current versions of HP's flavor of Unix[29] (HP-UX), the operating system automatically detects PA-RISC applications and directs them to run under the control of the Aries system with complete transparency.
- All IPF HP-UX releases will support applications that run on its companion PA HP-UX release. HP has performed benchmarks comparing the performance of applications running native on PA-RISC to that of the same applications running under Aries on Itanium-based systems of comparable performance.
- Testing has also shown that for many system-intensive applications, Aries and Itanium will deliver performance that is near to or equivalent to native performance on comparable PA-RISC systems.

29.   Unix is a registered trademark of The Open Group.

CHAPTER 13

Itanium Transition from IA-32

"Itanium will affect the folks who build applications... ISVs such as PeopleSoft and SAP, and even the casual developers. Also [Itanium will affect] the folks who use these application-enterprises as well as individuals who benefit from the use of computing-both the direct beneficiaries, like people who know they are using the computer, as well as indirect ones. Itanium...is going to have a very, very significant impact on the [technology] industry at large."

—Rajiv Gupta, HP Technical Lead on the IA-64 Processor Family

In this Chapter:

- Technical issues
- The business issue
- Itanium-related solutions to these issues
- Targeted clients for SAP R/3 resolution
- How does Itanium make these services compelling to the IA-32 customer?

The research and development labs at Hewlett-Packard, under chief scientist Joel Birnbaum, played a leading role in the creation of the PA-RISC architecture. The labs remained active in computer architecture research and soon recognized that PA-RISC was beginning to founder under the pressures of parallel processing. This pressure was exemplified by the issues that IA-32 machines were encountering

117

while running resource intensive applications like SAP. These issues fell into two categories: technical and business-related.

The Technical Issue

Arguably, the core technical problem stems from the fact that SAP R/3 pushes the envelope in the Windows environment. Microsoft Windows[30] is a 32-bit operating system that quickly hits limits in capacity for applications like SAP. The current 64-bit UNIX[31]-based systems have been the choice of CIOs and IT managers because of the broader memory addressability and inherent scalability in performance. Also, there has been a known ceiling in Windows performance that results from a combination of crunching the database with a maximum number of algorithms, and functionalities, such as limitations on the amount of throughput that is made available.

Compounding this is the all too common characteristic of a technical environment that is designed with a band-aid approach to solving problems. In this environment, extensive workarounds no longer extend the life of a Windows-based environment but become problems in and of themselves. For example, one major customer spent $18 million over a period of a year and a half to implement SAP. It was able to get only a fraction of the functionality up and running under the Windows environment.

The entire purpose of SAP is a complete and holistic system to manage a Fortune 500 business—and what the company got was essentially an $18 million version of QuickBooks on steroids. As a result, companies who have maximized Windows scalability are looking at UNIX as the way to grow their infrastructure.

However, a lingering customer perception is that the GUI (graphic user interface) nature of Windows makes it more cost effective and less complex to implement and administer. They also believe that UNIX is more expensive and difficult to manage, despite the repeated studies showing that it is highly scalable and reliable. As they process this decision, the need to grow their business is pushing them toward UNIX as a solution that will allow their IT environment to grow.

The Business Issue

From a business perspective, the limitations of SAP R/3 on Windows make it difficult for businesses to add functionality that would improve customer relationships and supply-chain efficiency. New modules of SAP R/3 and the new dimension products from SAP consistently require more power than customers currently get from the Windows platform.

---

30.   Microsoft and Windows are registered trademarks of Microsoft Corporation.
31.   UNIX is a registered trademark of The Open Group.

This is typical of complex production environments where it is difficult to supply what the users need if they prefer a Windows environment. To return to the example of the company that spent $18 million to get only the most basic SAP functionality, it's obvious that the technical and business problems are linked.

Are Windows-based solutions cheaper than UNIX solutions? It may seem that way on the books, but the attitude of overcoming performance with mass—by simply adding more servers down the line—is a sure path to disaster. This turns into an increasing spiral of technical problems, such as how to synchronize data on ever more servers, and business problems, such as where to continually get the capital needed for further equipment outlays.

Itanium-Related Solutions to These Issues

Due to the limitations in scalability under Windows, SAP customers are doing workarounds, customizing and changing configurations to meet business needs. The problems with relying on workarounds include the following:

• The high cost of custom development.
• Increased maintenance and administrative cost.
• Difficulty doing root cause analysis.
• Potential downtime and lost revenue, particularly with mission-critical applications.

One attempt to follow through on this model involved one of the largest nursery supply chains in the United States. Given its fast rate of acquiring smaller companies, the company specifically stated that fast scalability was its main priority. However, its choice of Windows for its servers ended up costing the company. When it began to hit performance snags, it was going to take at least two months to come up with solutions, while the business transactions were simply not being expedited in an efficient manner—if at all.

Another way to put it is to look at the problems addressed in the development of separate instances of SAP under an all-in-one-box Itanium server running SAP. They include the following:

• Resolving the difficulty keeping transports and data in sync.
• Breaking the lack of information integration.
• Reducing complex and costly administration.
• Reducing complex and costly patch and upgrade management.
• Eliminating difficulty making changes to meet new business requirements.

Targeted Clients for SAP R/3 Resolution

While any company using (or attempting to implement) SAP needs problems resolved, certain types of industries are more prone to issues relating to the software. This could be because they've run into a barrier in terms of scalability during a period of rapid growth, or it could result from instability due to a devotion to the Microsoft Windows environment.

Through experience in the field, it seems that the companies who stand to benefit the most are ones who are in the extended manufacturing industry, especially those doing process, discrete, or repetitive manufacturing. Or, to put it more simply, the industries that make complex "stuff," and the more complex, the more they stand to gain from a stable, fast system that can raise SAP's functionality for the company from 20 percent to 90 percent.

Given these characteristics, target markets include consumer products manufacturers, high-tech software developers, customers who make mill products, retailers, and those in the chemical and pharmaceutical industries. These companies often share similar characteristics.

First, they tend to have very specific requirements to have a complete supply-chain solution. For example, they'll often have a list of five or six SAP production modules that they need running, and by a very specific date or business quarter. If a CFO or CIO drives the solution, the time limit is often indicative of how long they'll be in the position if there is no effective resolution.

Second, challenges with the performance limitations in the Windows environment and the rising maintenance costs for customized workarounds in that environment soon take their toll. Complicating the desire to save money with a workaround is that these clients often have extremely complex production environments to work in, which makes a cut and dried method to work around an issue (such as throwing more servers at a problem) close to impossible.

Third, the transactions at risk in the SAP system are mission-critical. These are the transactions that potentially affect the key indicators of customer satisfaction and retention. Finally, these companies desire to scale into the future with fast transactions on the Web, such as with mySAP, and to provide a collaborative automated supply chain, such as with SAP APO.

How Does Itanium Help Make SAP a Better Solution for the IA-32 Customer?

Hewlett-Packard believes that the new Itanium[32] 2-based systems will create a "performance booster" for SAP R/3 on Windows and demonstrate why Itanium will assume a leadership position on Windows for enterprise customers. It should be able

---

32.   Intel and Itanium are registered trademarks or trademarks of Intel Corporation or its subsidiaries in the United States and other countries.

to do this for several reasons. First, the Itanium-based servers from HP will provide customers with the best performance and scalability for SAP R/3 on Windows. They have the best price–performance and most accurate ROI measurement for the overall implementation. Also, they have the most rapid, risk-free implementation for boosting Windows/SAP R/3 performance and scalability, providing the best path to new dimensions of SAP services.

The Itanium 2-based Server Performance Booster for Windows

The SAP performance booster server from HP provides industry-leading price–performance and the most accurate ROI measurement for the overall implementation. In addition, it provides the best performance and scalability for SAP R/3 on Windows. While it may not match the inherent stability of UNIX-based systems, this development alone provides a solid financial reason to make the move to Itanium-based systems.

Hewlett-Packard's proven experience in designing, building, integrating, and managing mission-critical environments enables HP to provide the highest availability and agility for Itanium-based servers in the SAP environment. In addition, HP's industry-leading service partnerships with SAP and Microsoft, and its SAP-specific tools, provide an optimized solution environment.

Given this boost in power and scalability, customers embark on the best path to SAP new dimension services. There is no better foundation for adding new SAP R/3 functionality and moving quickly to SAP BW, SAP APO, and SAP portals. The Intel Itanium processor's excellent performance for business intelligence makes it perfectly suitable for SAP BW, and its massive memory allocation opens up new horizons of scalability for SAP APO.

The Highest Level of SAP Partnership

As a SAP Global Alliance Partner, Hewlett-Packard also has the services and consulting to help customers to take advantage of the Itanium 2 performance booster on Windows. HP has established multinational SAP consulting capabilities, with trained and certified SAP consultants for optimal end-to-end solution creation, and extensive experience for rapid implementation and reduced project risk.

To achieve this level, all HP hosting solutions are certified by SAP, including 30 international operation service and data centers. HP is currently hosting SAP installations for over 130 SAP customers, providing accelerated time to productivity with minimal inhouse resources. Customers can focus on their business, while Hewlett-Packard takes care of their infrastructure needs.

In Summary

- The core technical problem stems from the fact that SAP R/3 pushes the envelope in the Windows environment. Microsoft Windows is a 32-bit operating system that quickly hits limits in capacity for applications like SAP. The current 64-bit UNIX-based systems have been the choice of CIOs and IT managers because of the broader memory addressability and inherent scalability in performance. Also, there has been a known ceiling in Windows performance that results from a combination of crunching the database with a maximum number of algorithms, and functionalities such as limitations on the amount of throughput that is made available.
- Companies who stand to benefit the most from Itanium-based systems are ones who are in the extended manufacturing industry, especially those doing process, discrete, or repetitive manufacturing.
- Hewlett-Packard's Itanium 2 server creates a performance booster for SAP R/3 on Windows and demonstrates why Itanium 2 servers will take early leadership in the market. HP provides customers with the best performance and scalability for SAP R/3 on Windows. It has the best price–performance and most accurate ROI measurement for the overall implementation. Also, it has the most rapid, risk-free implementation for boosting Windows/SAP R/3 performance and scalability.
- The SAP Itanium 2-based solution provides industry-leading price performance and the most accurate ROI measurement for the overall implementation. While it may not match the broad scalability of UNIX-based systems, this development alone provides a solid financial reason to make the move to Itanium.

Services for Transition

"Progress does not have to be disruptive and require massive reinvention and over-haul...HP's customers and partners get to keep the investments they have made as well as reap the benefits of the technological advances of the Itanium architecture."
—Jon Davis, Executive Summary of HP PA-RISC and
Itanium Architecture Compatibility

In This Chapter:

- Benefits for Itanium architecture early adopters
- Range of services supporting Itanium: Planning, porting, implementation, support
- Planning for Itanium
- Porting and migration: Choosing the best options
- Itanium implementation
- Support for IT investment

Although a move to an Itanium-based platform is justifiable on the basis of its unique combination of performance and price, any kind of upgrade to the IT environment is often viewed with suspicion as well as trepidation. However, Hewlett-Packard has never allowed a customer to work with technology without services designed to ease and encourage a smooth transition. HP offers a complete range of services to help customers move through the installation, porting, support, and education of IT staff in the new world of the Intel Itanium processor family.

Benefits for Itanium Architecture Early Adopters

A full suite of industry-leading services exists around HP's Itanium-based processors. Given the appeal of the Itanium architecture to the early adopters who are using it to push the boundaries of what they can do, many of the services are geared towards this customer segment, including services that support and aid a client's conducting development, porting, and migration activities.

Our inhouse Itanium architecture technical expertise enables early adopters to quickly understand the technology and the differences between Itanium and PA-RISC as well as IA-32.

By learning how to fully exploit the Itanium processor's capabilities stemming from its floating-point performance and EPIC architecture, early adopters can shorten the time to full implementation. Getting up to speed quickly allows these early adopters to utilize Itanium processors as a competitive advantage.

Range of Services Supporting the Itanium Processor

Hewlett-Packard offers its complete range of services and support up to and including Mission-Critical Services. Whether your company is looking to consolidate less powerful servers to a new Itanium server, implement a new SAP solution on the Itanium processor family, migrate from Solaris to Linux on the Itanium processor family, or simply replace a system with a new Itanium processor family system, HP has extended its services traditionally available on PA-RISC and IA-32 to include the Itanium processor family. The availability of these services facilitate this new technology's successful deployment in production as well as development environments, and a smooth transition repositions the IT infrastructure to take advantage of the Itanium processor's superior computing power. These services can be broken down into four major categories:

Planning

• IT architecture strategy/planning
• Implementation planning assistance for upgrading or migrating to Itanium-based systems
• Financing programs

Porting and Migration

• Porting and migration assessment workshop
• Detailed application porting and migration analysis
• Porting and migration implementation assistance

Implementation

- Itanium processor family-based system startup service
- Standard installation
- Full range of infrastructure services

Support

- Hardware support
- Software support
- Personalized system support
- Mission-critical support services

Planning for the Itanium Architecture

Consultants provided by Hewlett-Packard assist customers in their planning to attain optimum results with integrating Itanium processors into an enterprise's IT structure. Itanium systems implementation planning assistance provides a critical service for customers who want to own and manage the transition process to Itanium processor family technology. If the client requires assistance throughout the life cycle for technical or financial reasons, this service is especially valuable. Being able to define the customer as well as assist in transition planning processes is key to how Hewlett-Packard successfully provides this service to its clients.

HP Technology Finance's (HPTF) mission is to provide customers with financial acquisition and rental services that generate profitable asset growth. HPTF acts as a strategic enabler with differentiated financial offerings (utilities, bundles, garage). As a strategic enabler, HP is well positioned, being integrated into the overall value chain.

For example, HP's innovative, flexible financing programs and services can provide an influx of cash to a startup to establish an IT infrastructure or can offer financial structuring to an established enterprise to reduce IT costs and avoid technology obsolescence. HPTF enables customers to reduce the risk associated with investments in technology by providing convenient and flexible financial solutions that can improve their financial performance.

Customers expressing any of the following needs may benefit from an HPTF solution:

- Better match IT costs with the business benefits delivered by the IT solution (either revenue generation or cost savings).
- Reduce the financial and technological risk associated with investing in IT solutions.
- Hedge technology obsolescence.

- Match company depreciation policy with price–performance improvements (new generation introductions).
- Reduce IT costs and improve cash flow.
- Improve return on assets (ROA) by reducing assets through "off balance sheet" financing.

Porting and Migration: Choosing the Best Options

Given the high rate of change and technological improvements in today's marketplace, one of HP's most sought after services is SES, Software Engineering Services. This is due to its ability to help customers migrate their mission-critical applications to Itanium systems regardless of the operating system in use. Successful migration in this area achieves nothing less than the business objectives of the enterprise.

In doing so, the user can retain functionality of the existing or redesigned native enterprise applications. Due to the mission-critical nature of these applications, reducing the risk of transitioning to newer or emerging technologies is a major benefit. Also, integrating these existing applications with emerging e-solutions improves their usefulness, which shows up on the bottom line.

Hewlett-Packard provides assessment of their business applications, databases, and data for customers concerned about what a porting and migration project might mean given their existing resources. The assessment includes consideration of business drivers and the impact of change—a clear picture of what it will take to successfully complete the porting process of the most important applications.

Itanium Architecture Implementation

The HP Itanium System Startup Service accelerates and simplifies the evaluation process and planning for future implementation of Itanium-based servers. It also provides this same service for the related hardware, operating systems, and software. As one of the two generators of the Itanium processor architecture, HP is well positioned to assist organizations in gaining the greatest advantage from the processor's implementation.

An expert engineer with Hewlett-Packard's Itanium System Startup Service typically delivers the new servers directly to a customer's site. Typically, the implementation has two major components. First, it contains system configuration assistance and orientation. Second, it provides for planning for future implementations of additional servers.

System configuration assistance covers integrating the new server into a customer's existing networks. This includes setting up the proper file structure, defining user profiles, allocating accounting procedures, interfacing storage systems, and establishing standard operational procedures. The HP engineer can also provide assistance for both installing and configuring the application software on the new Itanium-based server.

While on site, the HP engineer provides orientation and planning assistance to ensure that the Itanium processor technology is utilized quickly and efficiently. This part of the service gives the customer's IT staff knowledge about the unique capabilities of the Itanium processor and the operating system that are not available on other platforms. This has the benefit of leveraging HP's vast knowledge and development experience with the Itanium-based platform. It simplifies integration of the new Itanium-based server with existing networks and also provides the following additional benefits:

- Customized configuration of the Itanium-based server and HP-UX or Linux operating system.
- Orientation to Itanium technology for IT staff.
- Planning document for migrating applications to Itanium-based servers.

Standard Implementation Services

IT performance is optimized by HP's Data Center Services through two main methods: improving existing IT facilities and building the physical aspects of new data centers. Although an overwhelming majority of businesses depend heavily on their IT infrastructure, it may be housed in a facility not designed for the solution components—for example, in areas that are prone to overheating or that have improper fire prevention equipment to safeguard the servers.

Often, IT organizations would like to build new data centers or improve existing ones to accommodate business growth, increased need for server power, or changes in the business structure. Companies adding new technology often need to remove or rearrange existing equipment, but may not have the time or expertise to tackle this type of project. Data Center Services assists in site preparation and verification. In these cases, HP reviews a computing environment for characteristics such as floor weighting, power, accessibility, and cooling to ensure that customers' equipment will operate properly over the long term.

Global Deployment Management Services

After a major new IT solution has been designed, the next need is to determine how it should be physically delivered and installed. The nature of the solution influences its complexity and the way the implementation should be managed. For example, client/server architectures, common desktop environments, site network set ups, and point-of-sale and messaging solutions often cannot be implemented all at one time.

This implementation model often requires repetitively building and installing a significant number of similar hardware and software configurations. Typically, these need to be customized for each client. They are then made available to
many users in a planned and coordinated manner, across multiple sites, countries,
and regions.

This deployment phase can then be highly complex and costly to handle, and
includes many potential risks to the success of the total solution implementation
phase. Hewlett-Packard works with customers with a dedicated set of global integration and installation services and capabilities that specifically address global volume
solution rollout needs, which is especially helpful in cases when offices are geographically remote.

Integration, Onsite, and Relocation Services

The integration and installation services available at HP make it much easier
for customers to develop and implement systemwide solutions. These services
include solution verification, implementation model planning, and factory integration. This also allows for the staging, testing, and consolidation of Itanium hardware
and software.

Customers that cannot tie up IT resources or those with limited staff often find
it challenging to add new hardware to their computing environment. Luckily, HP's
Onsite Services provide an answer to this dilemma. HP's experienced field installation teams offload IT staff while ensuring that equipment is up and running quickly
and reliably.

HP Relocation Services offers complete management of equipment relocation
activities at a single fixed price, an especially important point for cost-conscious clients. The relocation of IT systems or data centers can be as simple as moving a piece
of equipment across the floor or as complicated as moving an entire data center
overseas. In these cases, HP acts as the single point of contact and manages all
diverse activities and complex resources necessary to successfully implement and
conclude a customer's IT equipment relocation.

Support for IT Investment

The HP System Support Service provides high-quality support that enables organizations to increase equipment uptime. This in turn reduces any drops or gaps in productivity. It promotes the flexibility to choose response times and coverage periods
that meet specific service needs.

Hardware Support

HP provides both onsite and remote hardware support. An assigned customer
engineer or contract administrator is always available to meet support needs.

They're available to provide environmental surveys. Additionally, they can install add-on Itanium products and provide preventative hardware maintenance.

Each of these items serves to increase system uptime. It also gives clients the highest quality support for locations worldwide. By providing an escalation management system and meeting support needs cost effectively, it increases the return on the initial IT investment in Itanium-based architecture.

Software Support

Hewlett-Packard offers comprehensive software support for HP-UX, Linux, and Microsoft Windows environments. Technical experts at HP's Response Centers are available to provide first-line support and software assistance. Clients normally obtain this service by telephone help-line or by online question submission.

Similarly, HP makes software updates available for HP-UX, Linux, and Microsoft operating environments. Updates can be shipped out on CD-ROM directly to a client. Of course, the vast majority of these updates are available in self-installing packages online at the appropriate online site. (See Appendix B for a list of Web-related links.)

Mission-Critical Support Services

Mission-Critical Support Services ensure high availability through a comprehensive mission-critical support solution of preventative and rapid reactive services. HP Critical Systems Support (CSS) is the optimal level of support when business is dependent on critical applications and is severely affected by unplanned downtime. CSS provides technical expertise through an integrated combination of proactive services and fast problem resolution to meet the demands of any computing environment.

Education

Education provided by HP can serve to bridge the gap between what you know now and what you need to know to help understand and optimize Itanium technology. The courses help programmers and IT administrators become familiar with Itanium architecture and with the operation of Itanium-based environments for HP-UX, Windows, and Linux. The curriculum is designed to be complementary with the other Itanium-based services offered by HP to help clients make the right choices for their IT needs.

In Summary

- Many of the available services are geared towards the early adopter customer segment. This includes services that support and aid a client's conducting development, porting, and migration activities.

- The services provided for Itanium architecture fall into four major categories: planning, porting, implementation, and support.
- Strategy/planning consultants provided by Hewlett-Packard assist users in their planning to attain optimum results when implementing Itanium-based systems into the firm's IT structure. They can determine the best strategy for integrating Itanium into the existing infrastructure for maximum business results.
- Successful porting and migration achieves nothing less than the business objectives of the enterprise. In this manner, the customer can retain functionality of the existing or redesigned native enterprise applications. Reducing the risk of transitioning to newer or emerging technologies is a major benefit.
- The HP Itanium System Startup Service accelerates and simplifies the evaluation process and planning for future implementation of Itanium-based servers. It also provides this same service for the related hardware, operating systems, and software.
- The HP System Support Service provides high-quality support that enables organizations to increase uptime for both hardware and software. This in turn reduces any drops or gaps in productivity.

CHAPTER 15

Compilers in the Itanium/ EPIC Architecture World

"With the capabilities in the Trimaran [compiler], you are able to go in an aggregate large chunks of code, and kind of undo the modularity that we've all been told in computer science is a good thing. That gives you a broader base from which to compile, so that you can understand and put more code together."
—Tom Christian, HP Labs Scientist, in *Electronic Engineering Times*

In This Chapter:

- Instruction-level parallelism (ILP) compilers
- Improved parallelism from EPIC
- Compilers under EPIC
- EPIC specifications for developers
- The Trimaran compiler

The Intel Itanium[33] processor family comes as a milestone in the continuing evolution of microprocessors. It is the first enterprise-class 64-bit processor that has the power to become pervasive because of its aggressive price/performance ratio. A number of its awesome performance characteristics come from its ability to use the

33. Intel and Itanium are registered trademarks of Intel Corporation or its subsidiaries in the United States and other countries.

new, explicit forms of parallelism under its EPIC architecture and from its strong, optimized compilers.

Instruction-Level Parallelism (ILP) Compilers

In the age of CISC computers, there was no significant ILP available to the user or compiler. Most compilers of the era were merely an enabler for the higher maintainability and convenience of high-level languages, but the developer had to pay a performance price for not using assembly language.

Early RISC processors first began exposing ILP. With nonstalling loads and exposed branch latencies, the role of the compiler in performance began to increase. As the RISC era progressed, instruction scheduling became increasingly important to performance.

However, the RISC architectures severely restrict the compiler's ability to express the available parallelism. With EPIC, the compiler has the architectural tools to express far more parallelism. It becomes the driving force in realizing the performance potential of the underlying hardware.

Problems with Today's Processors

Today, 32-bit servers or proprietary 64-bit RISC servers are the norm. They have respectable price/performance ratios but are either fundamentally limited in performance scalability or are exceedingly expensive.

Servers based on the Intel-architecture 32-bit (IA-32) processors, for example, are unable to address large amounts of memory. Meanwhile, 64-bit RISC architectures have the necessary performance and addressing, but they are more expensive and generally lock the customer into a proprietary operating environment and a single computer vendor.

End users and IT professionals alike are clamoring for high performance and large addressing at an economical price. And they also are asking for pervasiveness so that they do not have to deal with multiple architectures and complexity.

HP and Intel co-developed the Itanium processor family architecture. The result is a high-performance, parallel 64-bit architecture that has the performance headroom to grow in the future and can be priced at a level to ensure its widespread adoption. The Itanium architecture fulfills both of these promises and is likely to become pervasive very quickly.

Improved Parallelism from EPIC

The Itanium architecture uses every practical technique to increase parallelism, or the ability to execute multiple instructions during each machine cycle. Parallelism improves performance because it allows more instructions to be carried out at once.

The architecture of the Itanium processor family is designed not only to take advantage of parallelism, but to do it explicitly.

The whole *raison d'etre* of the EPIC architecture is to make absolutely certain that as many instructions per cycle as possible are executed and to ensure that the compiler has the available resources to sustain this high rate of completion. And although all processors face penalties if an instruction is incorrectly executed or scheduled, these are minimized in the Itanium processor, reducing their effect on parallelism.

This is the design philosophy at the heart of the EPIC. The EPIC philosophy is a big reason why Itanium processors are so different from other 64-bit processors. This newly developed architecture provides much higher levels of ILP without unacceptable increases in hardware complexity.

Compilers Under EPIC

How does EPIC achieve such excellent performance? It does so by placing the burden of finding parallelism squarely on the compiler. It is true that processor hardware can pull out parallelism in a limited form. However, it is more efficient and speedier to let the compiler find the instances of parallelism explicitly. Since a compiler can see the whole code stream, it can make global optimizations as it runs through the code.

The compiler communicates this parallelism explicitly to the processor hardware. It does this by creating a three-instruction bundle that it issues to the hardware with directions on how the instructions should be executed. The hardware focuses almost entirely on executing the code as quickly as possible.

The Challenges of Object-Oriented Code

The predominance of object-oriented code has presented developers and compiler designers with a series of challenges. Under this form of coding, there are many small procedures. Even more importantly, of these procedures, many more are indirect, or virtual, procedures. This development limits the absolute size of regions and bounds the scope for ILP. Since this style of code is inherently serial, items must be checked before executing a load or store.

Solutions to the Challenges of Object-Oriented Code

The Itanium processor's unique EPIC architecture allows us to do something we call *inlining* of code. Speculative inlining and execution is the most common variant of this. Basically, if you've got a piece of code that does not have a virtual address, but you know the address, the compiler can look at this, and even though it's broken into small procedures, it can look at the procedures as a sequence or serial set of procedures. It can put them in line so that it can look at these procedures as one long block of executable code.

Where you actually have a problem is when you don't actually know that the procedure is in that line. In other words, the address gets computed as part of the execution of the program. But in this case, you can speculate. The compiler will speculate that the code will go to a certain block, so it will be placed in line for now.

If the code doesn't go there, the compiler can use the control speculation aspect of the EPIC architecture to correct the error. It won't generate a fault or crash but instead will self-correct on the fly. This guarantees correct exception behavior and shows how architectural support for speculation can ensure a system's recoverability.

The Compiler: Key to Performance in EPIC

Research has shown time and again that the most efficient method to improve parallelism is to let the compiler find the instances explicitly. The compiler contribution to total performance is steadily increasing. In part this is the result of the increased pipelines, wider issue bandwidth, and longer latencies, especially in regard to memory.

Since the compiler views the total code stream, it can make global optimizations as it runs through the code. This also takes advantage of the new architectural features available in the compiler, such as speculation and predication. Given the new centrality of the compiler to the performance issue, HP at the time of the Itanium-based product introduction supports five native compilers, as shown in Figure 15–1.

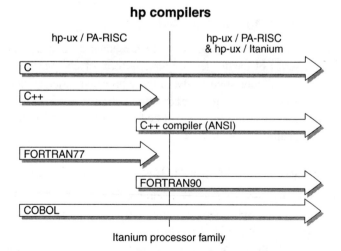

Figure 15-1   HP's Five Supported Native Compilers

EPIC Specifications for Developers

EPIC has tremendous flexibility in being able to run both little-endian and big-endian applications and operating systems. Because it can run applications on Windows,[34] Linux,[35] and HP-UX, there are immediate and obvious cost savings on porting issues. It's also worth noting that there are a number of features built into the new EPIC architecture that will be of special note to developers and coders. These features start with an advanced floating-point architecture.

This is a major opportunity for developers of technical software. Itanium can offer 128 80-bit floating-point registers. It can also perform single, double, and extended-double precision floating-point operations in parallel—so it gives you precision as well as speed. Further enhancements in this area include software pipelining, fused multiple-add instruction, and rotating registers.

Another advantage is that HP's libraries for the HP-UX operating system take full advantage of the company's industry-leading knowledge of EPIC's architecture. A whole suite of improvements that have resulted in this include:

- MLIB: A collection of subroutines that provide frequently used mathematical software for scientific and technical computing that Itanium excels in.
- libm: An optimized floating-point math library for C, C++, and Fortran 90 that was designed with Itanium's fast, accurate, and functional next generation of architecture in mind.
- Vector Math Library: A set of algebraic and transcendental functions that have been developed as part of a joint project between HP and CERN. These have been optimized to deliver high precision and unmatched performance for vector-applied calculations.
- HP MPI: A high-performance implementation of the message-passing interface for the Itanium architecture that gives developers both an API and a software library to support efficient and portable parallel message-passing applications. This makes it ideal for a clustered enterprise environment.

In addition, the new architecture contains 128 integer registers, 64 predicate registers, 128 central registers, and 8 branch registers. This allows low-latency storage space of intermediate results in complex calculations, efficient loop parallelization, and advanced branch production. Also, this improves branch intensive code performance. It improves this performance by using predication that uses conditional execution to smooth out branches. This allows the system to minimize the penalty of mispredicting results.

---

34.   Microsoft and Windows are registered trademarks of the Microsoft Corporation.
35.   Linux is a registered trademark of Linus Torvalds.

The compiler's complete view of the source code, combined with 'profiling,' allows the compiler to provide fast optimization while highlighting potential bottlenecks that may exist within the code itself. These bottlenecks in turn will be able to be reduced by regressive analysis. Today's compilers are already showing performance gains, and this will only improve as updates and improvements are incorporated into future versions.

The Trimaran Project

In 1998, Hewlett-Packard established the Trimaran project, which was completed as part of a consortium of three different universities' computing departments. HP released directly to the universities compiler information, especially as it related to HP-UX, around the EPIC concepts and asked them to develop a new compiler based on its precepts. The release of this research compiler that is billed as an academic "infrastructure" was aimed at enabling universities to develop compiler technology for EPIC.

Compilers have always been a crucial part in making PA-RISC work as well as it has. However, the move into the EPIC architecture and meeting the challenges of object-oriented code quickly made HP realize that compilers were immensely more important. Because of this, HP predicted that the time spent releasing the compiler for testing would pay off 5 years in the future—it was very much correct in that prediction.

In addition to HP's own lab work, the Itanium architecture has benefited from 4 years of development and testing done on these campuses. By any standards, the testing has been rigorous and thorough. In fact, an estimated 100 million lines of code have been run through the compilers in development across HP-UX, Windows, and Linux—creating a compiler with unmatched maturity in the development cycle that is ready for prime time in the new EPIC architecture.

One of the major benefits of working directly with Intel is that Hewlett-Packard gained more experience working with compilers. Instead of working with a single operating system and creating applications for it, HP was able to release over 100 different applications in three different operating systems.

The current HP-UX compilers are extremely mature for this point in the development cycle of a new architecture. They also come with many of the qualities that make them ideal for work in the EPIC world:

• Ability to vary parameters such as the instruction width.
• An emulator that can execute code for detailed simulations performance.
• A source-level environment.
• A code generator.
• Full support for predication and speculation.

• A suite of optimization modules, enabling tasks such as loop unrolling and global scheduling.

It's predicted that the up and coming Itanium processors will alter and reshape cooperation between the hardware and the compiler. EPIC architecture itself will contain a large number of execution units. The compiler will organize instructions into specific data streams that can be simultaneously executed. Because of this, compilers that comprise the specific qualities that the Trimaran project put forward will be very much in the driver's seat when it comes to the Itanium processors' ultimate performance.

In Summary

• Early RISC processors first began exposing ILP. With nonstalling loads and exposed branch latencies, the role of the compiler in performance began to increase. As the RISC era progressed, instruction scheduling became increasingly important to performance.
• HP and Intel co-developed the Itanium architecture. The result is a high-performance, parallel, 64-bit architecture that has the performance headroom to grow in the future and can be priced at a level to ensure its widespread adoption. The Itanium architecture fulfills both of these promises and is likely to become pervasive very quickly.
• The newly developed EPIC architecture provides much higher levels of ILP without unacceptable increases in hardware complexity. EPIC achieves such excellent performance by placing the burden of finding parallelism squarely on the compiler.
• Itanium's unique EPIC architecture allows inlining of code. Speculative inlining and execution is the most common variant of this. The compiler can look at many small procedures and put them in line so that it can look at these procedures as one long block of executable code.
• EPIC has tremendous flexibility in being able to run both little-endian and big-endian applications and operating systems. There are a number of features built into the new EPIC architecture that will be of special note to developers and coders. These features start with an advanced floating-point architecture.
• The current HP compilers are extremely mature for this point the in development cycle of a new architecture. They also come with many of the qualities that make them ideal for work in the EPIC world.

The Secure Sockets Layer

"Hewlett-Packard holds a leadership position in the emerging market in Web server security. With its complete solution portfolio that includes such proven software products as Virtualvault, Webproxy, and Webenforcer, hardware products, appliances and consulting services, HP's cross-platform security solutions offer strong customer benefits for protecting Web servers and associated applications."

—Chris Christiansen, VP of Internet Infrastructure and
Security Software at IDC (April, 2001)

In This Chapter:

- The need for security without slowdowns
- The Secure Sockets Layer (SSL)
- SSL demands on processing power
- Reasons for Itanium's outstanding performance
- Who benefits from Itanium speed for SSL transactions

The explosive growth in electronic commerce has led to a rash of new concerns, mostly regarding privacy and security when it comes to the transfer of funds or sensitive information. As a result, the need to provide secure Web transactions has also increased. During each and every transaction that is made online, it's likely that the data is kept secure by the Secure Sockets Layer (SSL).

The Need for Security Without Slowdowns

The primary idea to remember while surfing online in this day and age is that the World Wide Web is much like the Wild Wild West—a complete free for all. When you're on the Internet and clicking on Web pages and HTML pages, you're basically out in the open and vulnerable. People can use "sniffing" software to track where you visit and gather potentially sensitive information about you. Because of this, it's increasingly important to protect personal as well as financial information while on the Internet.

Therefore, the two most important aspects of information transfer over an open network are security and speed. On its face, these two needs may actually seem immutable, for encryption and decryption take additional time and CPU cycles. Complicating this equation is the raised expectations of the clientele, who are now used to quick load times and broadband versus dial-up modem connections.

With a slow system, the end user may have to select the request button multiple times. Worse, they may even give up and leave the site before the transaction is completed. The revolutionary architecture of Itanium gives you an edge in both areas—security, but without sacrificing speed in the process.

The Secure Sockets Layer

SSL technology was first developed by Netscape in 1994, then standardized by the Internet Engineering Task Force (IETF) in 1996. SSL is a security protocol that provides private communication over the Internet or a corporate intranet. Its purpose is to allow client and server applications to communicate in such a way as to prevent eavesdropping, tampering, or message forgery. It does this by encrypting data carried by transport protocols such as Transmission Control Protocol (TCP).

The Two Layers of SSL: Record and Handshake

SSL itself is composed of two layers: the Record Protocol and the Handshake Protocol. The Record Protocol makes sure the connection is private, using symmetric cryptography such as Triple Data Encryption Standard (3DES) or RC4 (Ron's Code 4—an RSA variable-key-size encryption algorithm developed by Ron Rivest). It also ensures that the connection is reliable, using secure hash functions such as Secure Hash Algorithm (SHA) or Message Digest 5 (MD5—a one-way hash algorithm) for keyed message authentication code (MAC) computations.

The Handshake Protocol allows the server and client to authenticate each other by utilizing asymmetric or public key cryptography such as Rivest-Shamir-Adleman (RSA) encryption or electronic data handling (EDH). This authentication process, known as *handshaking,* allows the server and client to negotiate a shared secret that is secure. This in turn ensures that the communicated negotiation is reliable.

SSL Events

During any transaction completed over the Internet—whether it is a consumer purchasing online or two dotcoms completing a transfer of data—the first step is to establish a connection through the Internet. This is the part known as the handshake. If it is to be a security-conscious transaction, the initial contact can be passed on to a secured connection. The URL sometimes indicates whether a transaction is secure: The unsecured connection is labeled *http://* and the secured one is denoted by *https://*.

When the need for security is established, encryption and decryption starts to take place on the back end of the Web server. All data coming from the user is encrypted and then decrypted only on the receiving server—as though a virtual private network exists for this one secured connection. This is demonstrated in Figure 16–1.

The downside is that it is a huge drain on CPU cycles. The difference in processing power needed between secured and unsecured transactions is substantial.

SSL Demands on Processing Power

SSL transactions require a great deal of computing power to encrypt and decrypt information being passed over the Internet. A server that can easily process over 1,000 unsecured transactions can find itself bogged down handling only 50 to 60 secure transactions. There are several reasons for these performance issues.

To begin with, establishing an SSL connection with the 1,024-bit encryption required takes 10 times longer on average than an unsecured Web transaction. This problem is compounded by the nature of Internet traffic.

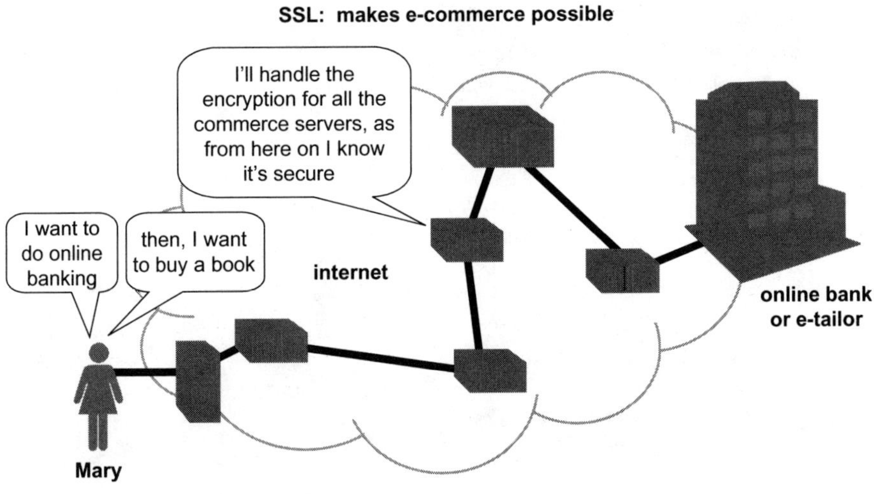

Figure 16-1   SSL Transaction Process

Instead of a steady state of a bell curve of usage, the pattern tends to run in sudden bursts in usage. The traffic created by these bursts can be more than 10 times the ordinary flow. During these high-traffic periods, the server can drop requests so that access is slow or simply denied to users seeking to close transactions. These issues are listed graphically in Figure 16–2.

The worst result can be felt on the bottom line: lost revenue caused by missed opportunities and aggravated users. In an extreme example, the delay of making an online stock trade at a brokerage service could mean a change in stock price that causes the client to lose hundreds of thousands of dollars. Obviously, the need for a microprocessor that can handle the additional loads of encryption and secure transactions is a critical one.

The SSL Benchmark

The parameter that measures SSL performance of a given processor is simply the number of secure transactions that can be handled per second. This benchmark encapsulates the entire SSL transaction, beginning with the external client, crossing the network to the server, traveling through the interrupt stack, network code, operating system, Web server, and cryptographic libraries to the data. Measurement of the performance time is not completed until the transaction crosses all the way back out again.

During benchmark tests, the best SSL performance was obtained with an Itanium-based server running Zeus Web Server software on the HP-UX operating system. This combination delivered almost 1,200 SSL transactions per second with a

SSL performance problem	causes of the problem
• Establishing an SSL connection takes too much CPU time • Web server must execute 1 RSA operation with its private key	• 1 RSA operation takes >10x longer than simple web connection
• Servers bog down when they receive bursts of SSL connection requests	• web sites may receive bursts of thousands of secure web requests in seconds

• The result is delays, or missed opportunities with customers
  • Users are one click away from the competition
  • The interruption is often at the most crucial point, order-taking
	• requests are queued up or dropped by the server

Figure 16-2   SSL Performance Issues

realistic SSL workload (1,024-bit RSA, 128-bit RC4, SHA, and 14-kB transfers). These results corroborate the trend detailed in Figure 16–3, which shows how Itanium performance outstrips other methods.

The results are clear: by using the power of Intel Itanium[36] microprocessors, clients can attain the twin goals of fast performance with the reliable security features equipped for an enterprise environment. In addition, HP-UX's roots in UNIX[37] allow it to provide the robust stability needed for mission-critical applications. Finally, the flexibility of HP-UX 11i can easily interface with Web application (application servers) and data center infrastructures.

Reasons for Itanium's Outstanding Performance

From the start, the Itanium processor family architecture was designed to be particularly strong at mathematical processes such as floating-point calculations. (For more details on the Itanium processor's strengths in this area, see Chapter 2). Specifically, the heavy lifting of a large integer processor family includes 64-bit capabilities, improved floating-point performance, large register set, and explicitly parallel design. These features enable Itanium processors to efficiently process cryptographic operations on-chip.

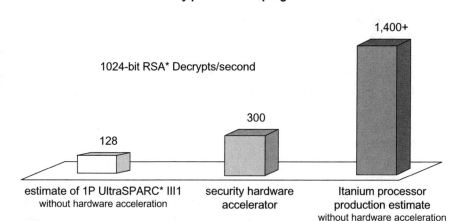

security performance progress

1,400+

1024-bit RSA* Decrypts/second

300

128

estimate of 1P UltraSPARC* III1
without hardware acceleration

security hardware
accelerator

Itanium processor
production estimate
without hardware acceleration

Figure 16-3   Itanium Security Performance Progress

---

36.   Intel and Itanium are registered trademarks of Intel Corporation or its subsidiaries in the United States and other countries.

37.   UNIX is a registered trademark of The Open Group.

This on-chip performance far outstrips an external cryptographic processor. Because an external processor would live "off the board," it would always have the disadvantage of having an additional communications bottleneck communicating with the primary processor.

In addition, the Itanium processor benefits from its architecture's ability to multiply efficiently. This ability is directly related to the SSL transaction rate. The expanded number of registers, pipelining, and reduced latency all play into the transaction rate increase. Furthermore, the processor clock rate directly scales with the SSL transaction rate. For example, a 550-MHz processor was found to be about 25 percent faster at SSL transactions than a 440-MHz processor of the same architecture.

Finally, the UNIX-based HP-UX 11i operating environment and associated software and Zeus Web Server act to project Itanium speed and power for security purposes. In each case, they have been tuned to eliminate bottlenecks that would prevent the performance power of the Itanium from reaching the user application.

Who Benefits from Itanium Speed for SSL Transactions

Faster performance at a reasonable price is a general benefit for all clients. However, the unique aspects that make Itanium especially desirable for SSL transactions confer a tremendous advantage on certain firms that depend disproportionately on these transactions for growth or revenue. These organizations include:

• Capacity-driven, hyper-growth xSPs.
• E-commerce companies generating millions of transactions.
• B2B or large data center enterprises in communications, finance, and extended manufacturing industries that are running millions of SSL transactions.
• Telecommunications companies who are expanding services to include Internet access, Web hosting, and other Internet offerings.
• Mobile service providers who are aggressively delivering new services for customers.

In Summary

• The two most important aspects of information transfer over an open network are security, and speed. On its face, these two needs may actually seem immutable, for encryption and decryption take additional time and CPU cycles.
• SSL is a security protocol that provides private communication over the Internet or a corporate intranet. Its purpose is to allow client and server applications to communicate in such a way as to prevent eavesdropping, tampering, or message forgery. It does this by encrypting data carried by transport protocols such as TCP.

- SSL transactions require a great deal of computing power to encrypt and decrypt information being passed over the Internet. A server that can easily process over 1,000 unsecured transactions can find itself bogged down handling only 50 to 60 secure transactions.
- The parameter that measures SSL performance of a given processor is simply the number of secure transactions that can be handled per second. During benchmark tests, the best SSL performance was obtained with an Itanium server running Zeus Web server software on the HP-UX operating system.
- Itanium processors benefit from its architecture's ability to multiply efficiently. This ability is directly related to the SSL transaction rate. The expanded number of registers, pipelining, and reduced latency all play into the transaction rate increase.

Hewlett-Packard's Scalable Processor Chipset

"Whatever computer you can build, people will take advantage of that situation...you can envision a system that's far more intelligent. It could be far more intelligent about everything. It could do all sorts of pattern matching about your last accesses and really understand so that you could ask queries against it. All sorts of great things that can come from millions more [CPU] cycles."

—Jerry Huck

In This Chapter:

• Chipset Differentiators
• The Next Generation Scalable Processor Chipset
• Chipset Capabilities
• Chipset objectives

The 64-bit world is rapidly changing by pushing the boundaries of price and performance unexpectedly far. Once the exclusive preserve of proprietary, high-margin RISC architectures, 64-bit processing is finally becoming pervasive across the technical and enterprise space. Part of this shift is that commoditization of 64-bit processors and the architectures that are built around them are very close indeed.

The HP zx1 Chipset is priced like a commodity part, but it has all the benefits of a chipset designed to meet the rigorous requirements of the enterprise. It leverages high performance but economically priced DDR SDRAM (Double data rate synchronous dynamic random access memory) for additional cost savings. This promises to revolutionize the IT world by being both fast and ubiquitous. It also sets the stage for this chipset becoming the next standard in computing power.

Chipset Differentiators

Hewlett-Packard developed the Itanium® architecture specification with Intel®[38] as part of a grand partnership. The chipset that resulted from this combination of skill sets produced key differentiators that set it apart from anything else. One such differentiator is Hewlett-Packard's variant of the UNIX®[39] operating system, HP-UX. This is the only enterprise-class version of UNIX available with the Itanium processor family.

The second differentiator is the HP zx1 Chipset. This chipset will allow HP to make a strong move into the workstation and <8-way server markets. Also, it will make the architecture ubiquitous by moving into the volume, or 'mass computing' market.

Finally, the HP zx1 Chipset stands out from the crowd by setting some historic firsts. For example, this is the first chipset to support a 64-bit processor while at the same time offering high bandwidth and low latency at a volume market price.

This chipset also is unique in that it attains major five goals:

1. Achieves very low latencies and high-bandwidth throughput.
2. Achieves a very balanced design, ensuring that there are no bottlenecks from memory bus to the PCI bus across the entire chipset.
3. Achieves excellent economies, both economies of design and of unit cost.
4. Provides unparalleled flexibility in the low-end thanks to its modular design, allowing a number of different configurations to weight the chipset towards workstation or server use.
5. Providing the best setting to showcase the power of the Intel Itanium processor because it was specifically designed for the processor by the company who co-developed the processor architecture with Intel. This not only allows the processor to perform to the highest potential by keeping its pipelines fed with data, it also adds to the price/performance story of Itanium because it is a low cost design.

---

38.   Intel and Itanium are registered trademarks of Intel Corporation or its subsidiaries in the United States and other countries.
39.   UNIX is a registered trademark of The Open Group.

The Next Generation Scalable Processor Chipset

Hewlett-Packard's Scalable Processor Chipset zx1 is the center of next generation Intel Itanium 2-based workstations and servers. It also provides the core of the enterprise servers that allow up to 4-way multiprocessing. A 'chipset' is a set of microchips, microchip controllers, buses and connectors that are defined and laid out on the circuit board of a workstation or server.

The chipset defines all the core functions of a system, including its scalability and expandability. Entirely designed by Hewlett-Packard and an exclusive differentiator, the HP Scalable Processor Chipset zx1 is the chipset that defines the roles and functionality of the HP Itanium 2-based systems. Some of the key features and benefits are listed in the table below.

Features	Benefits
High memory bandwidth, low memory latency	Top application performance; faster time to solution
High memory capacity Supports DDR SDRAM	Enables optimum performance for large models/databases and ensures good price performance ratio
AGP-4X	Enables high performance, 3D graphics in workstation configuration
Scalability	Enables HP to deliver a family of systems tuned to meet a variety of needs

Chipset Capabilities

HP's philosophy is to deliver features that customers want for a class of products, without compromising schedule, performance or cost. HP's approach can be described as "lean and mean." Rather than add every "bell and whistle," HP focused on including only those features that power users of 1-4 way workstations and servers will value. For example, memory mirroring is not a feature of the HP zx1. This is a feature that takes redundancy to a point beyond the sweet spot of 1-4 way system users.

It is the most robust, most stable Itanium 2 chipset in the industry. The HP zx1 chipset was the turn-on vehicle for the Itanium 2 processor in early 2001. At that time, Itanium 2-based systems with the HP zx1 chipset were running UNIX, Linux[®40] and Windows [®][41]XP. It also has a memory capacity as low as 512MB and with an upper limit of 256GB.

---

40.   Linux is a registered trademark of Linus Torvalds.
41.   Microsoft and Windows are registered trademarks of Microsoft Corp

The Target Market

HP's next generation Itanium 2-based workstations and servers are targeted at performance hungry markets—such as mechanical computer-aided design (MCAD), digital content creation (DCC), desktop computer-aided engineering (CAE), simulation/visualization, life sciences, research, secure web serving and business intelligence, that need huge memory space, leadership floating point performance—high memory and low latency. Furthermore, the affordable cost of the system will be extremely attractive to software developers and the education market.

One area where the chipset will excel is in large clusters of dual processor machines running Linux. There is demand for dense, dual-processor compute nodes with extreme floating point performance from national labs, and science and research institutions.

The HP zx1 Chipset supports HP-UX, Linux and Windows. HP-UX is the only enterprise UNIX OS available for Itanium® -based systems. Linux is popular in academic and scientific communities. Software developed on Linux can be deployed on both Linux and HP-UX.

Addressing Processor Infrastructure Needs

The HP zx1 Chipset addresses the volume Itanium processor infrastructure needs on several key fronts. It delivers all-important, world-class memory latency numbers that handily beat those of today's Itanium® systems. Intel has stated that users may see 1.5 to 2X performance increase over Itanium.

The HP Chipset zx1 is an ideal setting for the Intel Itanium 2 processor, because it complements the processor's price/performance. It will be of particular interest to the following clients:

- Customers who are looking for the best price performance ratio for a 64-bit workstation or server, such as customers who want large numbers of systems for clusters, like those found in national laboratories and universities.
- Customers who want leading performance from a workstation or a server that scales up to 4-way SMP.
- Customers who have applications that benefit from parallel performance or have high memory throughput requirements, such as those found in the CAE, secure web serving, or DCC markets.

Today's IA-32 chipsets generally allow less than 4GB/s of processor bus bandwidth. The Intel Itanium 2 processor allows 6.4GB/s of processor bus bandwidth, and the bandwidth benefits are preserved across the chipset to ensure that data availability is optimal.

Chipset Objectives

Early market penetration will be especially high in markets where the ability to address large amounts of physical memory is important. These include the early adopter markets such as Computer Aided Engineering, Life Sciences, in-memory databases, large key or complex algorithm cryptography. In short, those who do what we defined in Chapter 4 as 'Technical Computing'.

The High Bandwidth, Low Latency Chipset

The HP zx1 Chipset is a modular three-chip solution designed by HP to enable them to provide customers with a cost-effective, high bandwidth, and low latency 1- to 4-way workstations and servers based on the next generation Itanium processor family platform. This chipset enables HP to deliver features that power users want without compromising schedule, performance or cost.

Memory bandwidth is the rate at which data can be sent/received to/from the main memory. Bandwidth is needed to get the highest level of application performance. For 1-way and 2-way systems, the HP zx1 Chipset enables 8.5 GB/s. For 4-way systems, the chipset enables 12.8 GB/s.

Latency is the amount of time from when data is requested by a processor to the time it is received. In digital designs, a typical method for increasing memory bandwidth is to increase the number of pipeline stages, which causes an increase in latency. The HP zx1 Chipset's uncompromising design provides high bandwidth and low latency for Itanium 2-based systems from HP. The result is superior applications performance.

Historically, HP's strength has been to develop and tune systems to deliver the kind of performance that professionals demand. The HP zx1 Chipset was designed to provide the best performance for demanding applications that do not fit within the processor cache. The memory system design is the key to performance in these cases. Here, the zx1 memory bandwidth has been optimized with dual memory controllers to provide up to 12.8GB/sec in a 4-CPU system and 80 nS of open page latency in a 2-CPU system.

The right functionality is provided by the optimized memory capacity. At 48GB, HP's 4-way system provides three times the memory capacity of other chipsets AGP4X support is also available, which provides for full, 3D graphics performance. HP's zx1 supports AGP4X, which enables designers to choose the parts they need, and the numbers of these parts to meet their specific system design requirements.

Clustering

Another area where this chipset will shine is in the area of clusters. We are seeing a huge appetite for dense, dual processor compute nodes with extreme floating-point performance. Most of this demand is for clusters running Linux.

The HP zx1 chipset is ideally suited for this purpose. It combines its industry leading bandwidth with the Intel Itanium processor's powerful floating-point performance. This allows it to make extremely impressive speed gains on large dual-processor clusters.

The Three Central ASICs

This chipset provides the high degree of parallel performance that ensures fast results and better time-to-market. HP is seeing demand from numerous National labs and other science and research institutions. Many of these organizations want to consume thousands of Itanium processors in zx1-based systems because of the Linux support and industry leading latency chipset layout for two of our Intel McKinley processor products. The impressive technical gains can in part be attributed to the workings of the critical three ASICs that are part of the chipset (see Figure 17-1):

1. The HP zx1 memory and I/O controller, which was codenamed "Pluto".
2. The HP zx1 I/O adapter, which was codenamed "Mercury".
3. The HP zx1 scalable memory expander, which was codenamed "Mickey"

The HP zx1 Memory and I/O Controller

The controller connects to the processor bus. It contains both the memory controller and the I/O cache controller. It interfaces to the Itanium 2 processor bus and provides a low latency connection to DDR memory either directly or through zx1 Scalable Memory Expanders. This component can connect up to 12 Memory

hp chipset zx1 components

the hp zx1 chipset contains three modular components:	
zx1 mio	hp zx1 memory & I/O controller • connects to processor bus • contains memory controller • contains I/O cache controller

zx1 ioa	hp zx1 I/O adapter
	• single I/O adapter that supports:
	  - PCI
	  - PCI-X
	  - AGP

zx1 sme	hp zx1 scalable memory expander • optional component used to: • increases memory capacity • increases memory bandwidth

Figure 17-1   Important ASICs

Expanders for quadruple the base memory capacity at the same time that eight I/O adapters are handling 4GB/sec of I/O bandwidth.

The HP zx1 I/O Adapter

The adapter is a chip that is a scalable solution. It is designed to support PCI, PCI-X and AGP bus architectures. It provides a scalable I/O implementation for a wide variety of systems.

The HP zx1 Scalable Memory Expander

The expander is an optional component used to increase memory capacity (up to four times) and increase bandwidth to the main memory to 12.8 GB/s. Acting as a memory hub, it decreases the number of signal loads on the memory bus, thereby allowing the system to dial up its memory transfer rate. The trade-off of using the zx1 memory expander is the cost of the chips and their footprint together with a modest 25ns of additional memory latency relative to direct attach.

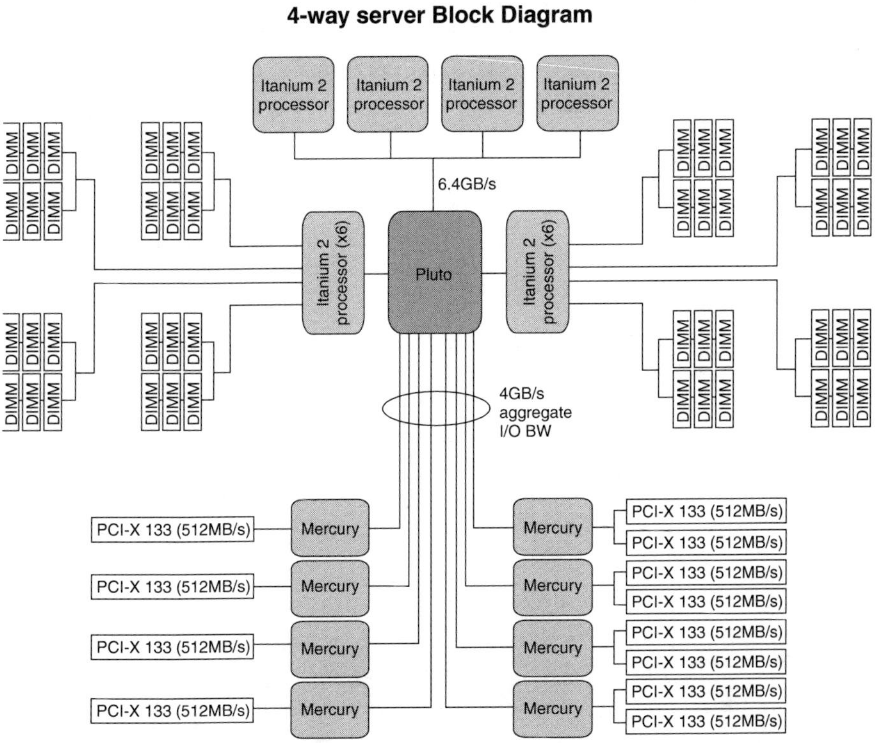

4-way server Block Diagram

Figure 17-2 The ZX1 Scalable Memory Expander

In Summary

- Hewlett-Packard's chipset is set apart from other systems in that it works with the only enterprise-class version of UNIX available with the Intel Itanium processor family, HP-UX.
- Also, this is the first chipset to support a 64-bit processor while at the same time offering high bandwidth and low latency at a volume market price.
- Hewlett-Packard's Scalable Processor Chipset zx1 is the center of next generation Intel Itanium processor workstations and servers with up to 4-way multiprocessing.
- HP's next generation Itanium-based workstations and servers are targeted at performance hungry markets—such as mechanical computer-aided design (MCAD), digital content creation (DCC), desktop computer-aided engineering (CAE), simulation/visualization, life sciences, research, secure web serving and business intelligence—that need huge memory space, leadership floating point performance, high memory and low latency.
- The HP zx1 Chipset is a modular three-chip solution designed by HP to provide customers with a cost-effective, high bandwidth, and low latency 1-to-4-way workstations and servers based on the next generation Itanium processor family platform. This chipset enables HP to deliver features that power users want without compromising schedule, performance or cost.

The Future of EPIC Processors and Systems

"If what you really need is the greatest scalability, the greatest future growth, the greatest performance and capacity in systems, Itanium will pull into the lead."

—Bill Worley

"Any form of technology, if sufficiently advanced, is indistinguishable from magic."

—Arthur C. Clarke

In This Chapter:

- Preexisting and continuing trends
- Where have the speed gains come from?
- The architectural lag—and opportunity
- Itanium Cache Size Development
- Benefits of the Compaq merger
- Complete security
- Fixed-issue machines

As we look ahead, there are really two directions that Hewlett-Packard and Intel are heading toward, due in large part to the development of the Intel Itanium processor family architecture.[42] One is a drive towards more performance—pushing

---

42. Intel and Itanium are registered trademarks of Intel Corporation or its subsidiaries in the United States and other countries.

the envelope and getting even more parallelism and more actions to be taken with every clock cycle of the CPU.

The other direction is driven less by technology and more by business economics. Other members of the Intel Itanium processor family will be created with an eye on filling out the marketplace by providing lower power consumption and lower cost members for applications that may not have the need for top speed. Instead, these chips will skew towards providing maximum value per dollar spent and maximizing the mips/watt of power consumed.

These two directions in turn are influenced by items that Itanium users in the enterprise computing environments would find important, which include:

- High reliability
- High availability
- Security

Preexisting and Continuing Trends

It's something of a cliché to say that to truly see where you are going, you need to look back at where you've been. However, it also happens to be very true in this case. If you take a look at Figure 18–1, you'll get a sense of one of the reasons why we chose to go to a new architectural design for the next generation of microprocessors.

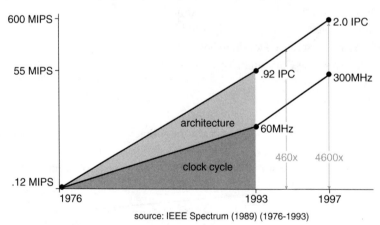

Figure 18-1 Microprocessor Performance Growth

Where Have the Speed Gains Come From?

Let's talk about what Figure 18–1 really shows. This chart is actually one driver for deciding that it was time to work on parallelism rather than clock speed to gain leverage in improving performance in the future. The observation was that up until 1993, the improvements in the performance growth came equally from clock cycle improvement, shrinking the chip die, and architectural improvements.

Speed gains from improving the architecture resulted in increasing the number of instructions that could be done per clock cycle. The gains moved from .045 from the early RISC machines in the 1970s to .92 per cycle. Note that an almost one instruction per cycle increase was reached at this time.

From the chart, it is obvious that on the hardware side and the architecture side, speed gains had increased almost 22 times. But what made us think that a new architecture was needed, and what actually led to the wholesale development of the next generation of architecture—EPIC—was that between 1993 and 1997, most of the improvements had come from the hardware side by shrinking the die and turning up the clock speed. The move from 60 MHz to 300 MHz was an almost 110-fold improvement.

The Architectural Lag—And Opportunity

On the architecture side, the gains had lagged at only a 42-fold improvement. And that was assuming that you actually could come close to having two instructions completed per cycle. This was a clear indicator to Hewlett-Packard that to attack the need for continued improvements, it needed to tackle the problem from the architectural side of things.

Hence, HP and Intel set about the development of the new architecture. Now that it has reached the point of deploying this new design in the marketplace, HP is very happy with the results. Instead of two instructions per cycle, it has pushed the boundaries to four and even six instructions per cycle. This has served to shift the dynamic of improving the chip so drastically that now it is looking at how to generate similar improvements from the hardware side again. This is where Hewlett-Packard will look to make the next breakthrough with this architecture.

Where Will Future Chip Enhancements Come From?

What this tells us is that looking ahead, the way we'll be able to get more powerful chips and expand Itanium's line into less power-consuming, value-laden chips will also change dramatically. The Intel Itanium processor family will actually take advantage of all the improvements that Intel, HP, and others, such as the former Compaq Alpha design team, have used to improve on CISC and RISC architectures. Again, the emphasis will return to reducing the chip's die size, increasing clock speeds, and the ability to place more transistors on a chip.

We'll be looking at the same new technologies we used to improve RISC and CISC designs to further this direction. Copper technologies, silicon on insulator technology—all of the things that can be done from a manufacturing process approach for RISC—can be applied to EPIC.

Dual or Multiple Chip Cores

In the RISC area, some vendors have come out with dual-core dies. The possibilities of putting two CPU cores on one chip and building it into a system are particularly striking. There is no reason why this technique could not be implemented on the Intel Itanium processor family as well.

Finding EPIC's "Sweet Spot"

As a new architecture emerges, it tends to fill the entire market space; that is, the first chip that comes out with the new technology usually tries to be all things to all markets. Normally, the design center of the architecture becomes more apparent as applications are developed to run on it. Eventually, the new architecture finds its "sweet spot," where it is king of its segment.

It won't take long for EPIC to find its own sweet spot in the microprocessor market. Likely, this will be at the high end of the marketplace, the segment where price is less of an issue when speed and scalability are the key success factors. RISC-based and CISC-based microprocessors will continue to coexist with EPIC designs, and they will dominate the middle to the lower end of the market in the near future.

EPIC may eventually dominate but not totally replace older architectures, which remain amazingly resilient in the face of new and improved technologies. After all, CISC does date back to 1976, and it is still around. This is because CISC has found and maintained its own sweet spot in the marketplace and maintains its advantage there.

Cache Size, Cache Hierarchy, and Compiler Development

Other improvements center around increasing the level 1 (L1) and level 2 (L2) cache on the chip and further enhancing the compilers to take advantage of the cache and to find new ways to increase parallelism. The reason the cache size makes such a difference is that the cache memory is closest to the processor. The L1 cache has the shortest delay in loading data and instructions for the processor, and therefore anything loaded or stored in L1 will help to speed up the overall performance.

L2 is the next closest memory "bucket," and so on. Therefore, an obvious way to improve the next versions of the Intel Itanium processor family will be to increase the cache sizes. Developing the chip so that additional levels can reside on or nearer the CPU chip will improve performance as well. Splitting the cache into separate instruction and data locations could potentially give new speed gains.

There is a database software vendor today who has developed an application to take an entire database from the disk device and place it in a computer's main memory. This results in an astonishing 10-fold improvement in access speed. By that same analogy, it's easy to see that if you can move this data from the main memory and put it into the cache—and as close to the processor as possible—relative kinds of speed improvements are possible.

Compilers will be improved by the ability to make better use of the cache hierarchy. Today, the complier actually gives hints to the processor as to what to store in a given cache level. Improving these algorithms means additional efficiency as the processor makes more "right decisions" that will enable it to run more efficiently.

Most of Hewlett-Packard's compilers on HP-UX are quite mature today. HP has been working on these for several years, and the code for HP is highly tuned. However, in the Linux and Windows operating environments, the compilers still need to reach the same level of maturity as in the UNIX[43]-based environment. This is important because improving the compiler is yet another way to create a new speed gain from existing microprocessor technology. For example, the more parallelism that the compiler can find, locate, and call out to the microprocessor, the greater the performance gain.

Benefits of the Compaq Merger

Another direction to look in is the area of higher availability. In the course of Hewlett-Packard's merger with Compaq, it picked up some new and extensive high-availability technology. Again, given the reliance that enterprises today place on IT infrastructure, the usefulness of a system that simply does not go down at all is becoming more and more invaluable.

For example, the fault-tolerant systems from the former Tandem Corporation today function in environments where it is important to never lose a transaction. In a fault-tolerant environment, two computers run in parallel. If one fails, the other one picks up the load, backing up a little if needed to ensure that it collects any transactions that might have been dropped in the initial failure, and then continues on. This running in tandem was the main development that fueled the computer maker Tandem, which became part of Compaq, and hence part of Hewlett-Packard. The Intel Itanium processor family, with its machine-check architecture, is an ideal candidate for the next generation of these machines.

Today, we have software that actually watches our highly available systems and monitors sections or pages of memory where we may see degradations of performance. If you have a system that is running 24/7, there is no time to take the sys-

---

43.   UNIX is a registered trademark of the Open Group.

tem down to run maintenance on the machine or its memory. In future Itanium-based systems, we will be able to take advantage of the architecture to improve these kinds of high availability and reliability techniques.

For server consolidation, the ideal is one giant server running complete software environments in virtual partitions, down to and including a single CPU—this can be made possible by the Intel Itanium processor family. The idea of computing as a utility becomes a closer reality with a centralized system that can handle multiple users, multiple networks, and multiple operating systems, consolidating all operations, helped by virtual partitions that can be made completely safe from software defects.

More impressively, the systems will be able to reallocate these partitioned resources as the demands change. Dynamic flexibility is the key here. To be able to handle different operating environments and also act as a fluid, not a rigid, system so that the most processing power gets put where it is needed is quite a challenge but offers an equally worthwhile benefit.

Complete Security

Our vision on security is to create a secure software environment: one that is secure from the booting of the system to the running of the application. The users will know that they can trust the machine from the time they switch the power on.

With HP-UX, Hewlett-Packard expects to be able to build a secure kernel. The Itanium architecture allows increased levels of security. There are four privileged levels that system software writers can actually access to select the given level of security for programs and users. Some systems today have four levels of protection, but most lack the four separate protection keys that Itanium will carry.

This allows for a more compartmentalized system of security so that different levels can be tailored to specific parts of the software program and thwart crackers, hackers, and other malicious users who would like to crash the system.

'Green' Chips of the Future

Intel's public intention is clearly to continue releasing more processors with the Itanium architecture. The entire Itanium processor family will be moving towards a higher level of performance at the same or a similar level of cost. Intel has also indicated that it will be producing a series of Itanium microprocessors with a lower power consumption, presumably at a correspondingly lower cost.

These chips will be more "green" than the others. That is, they will use less electricity to run. They won't draw as much power from the AC line, thus generating less heat and requiring fewer fans. The OEM systems vendors like HP will act as fast followers of these trends and build computers that either operate with tremendous speed, with moderate speed for moderate prices, or with energy efficiency in

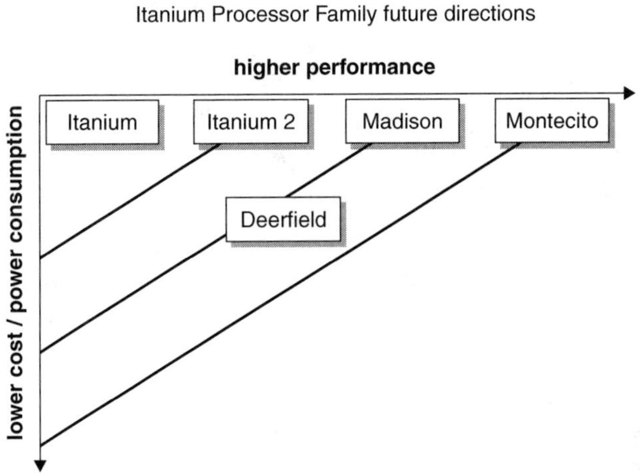

Itanium Processor Family future directions

higher performance

Figure 18-2 showing Itanium, Itanium 2, Madison, Montecito across the top with Deerfield below, arranged on axes of "lower cost / power consumption" (vertical) and higher performance (horizontal).

Figure 18-2 Itanium Processor Family Future Trends

mind. See Figure 18–2 below for a graphic representation of Intel's public roadmap sorted by these two trends.

Whichever trend proves to be the dominant is, in a way, actually irrelevant. What is key is that the entire IT world will be shaken to its very core by the rise of a new microprocessor that these two technology giants, HP and Intel, have created. In the final analysis, the business economics will favor a powerful, yet open industry standard architecture which is widely adopted by the industry over other proprietary options.

In Summary

- Now that Hewlett-Packard has reached the point of deploying the new design in the marketplace, it is very happy with the results. It has shifted the dynamic of improving the chip architecture so that now it is looking at generating future improvements from the hardware side again by shrinking the line sizes. Some of the potential improvements for future members of the Itanium family include enlarging the on-chip cache and even creating specific cache at different levels for instructions and data.

- A centralized system that can handle multiple users, multiple networks, and multiple operating environments brings us one step closer to the computing utility. Consolidating several servers onto one large machine, helped by virtual partitions that can run different operating environments, will be made possible by future generations of Itanium.

• Intel's public intention is clearly to continue releasing more processors with the Itanium architecture. The entire Intel Itanium processor family will be moving towards a higher level of performance at the same or a similar level of cost. Intel has also indicated that it will be producing a series of Itanium microprocessors with a lower power consumption and presumably at a correspondingly lower cost.

Technology Terms

Architecture   This term describes the internal structures of a microprocessor and how they work individually and together. Architecture is a term for the total design and design concepts. It also describes the assembly language instruction set of the microprocessor.

Central processing unit (CPU)   An older term sometimes used to refer to the microprocessor.

Complex Instruction Set Computer (CISC)   Intel Pentium processors are based on CISC architecture with the same elements of RISC included. CISC instructions are more complex and generally take multiple CPU clock cycles to execute. Not as many can be completed per second, but each instruction does more work in comparison to the more streamlined RISC instructions.

Compiler   A compiler interfaces between a programmer's high-level instructions and the hardware that can execute those instructions. The programmer writes code in a language such as C or C++. It is then put through a compiler, and the compiler analyzes the language statements and builds output code in a form that can be understood and executed by the system hardware. Before the Itanium processor family, it fell on the hardware to do the work of finding parallelism opportunities and optimizing them. This meant more chip complexity with less room for improving performance. With Itanium, the compilers now do that work. Itanium processor family compilers break regular sequential code into 128-bit sections with instructions attached telling the processor how the different instructions interrelate. This explicit expression of parallelism allows the processor to concentrate on executing parallel code as fast as possible, without further optimizations or interpretations. *See* Explicit Parallelism *and* Implicit Parallelism.

Endian   Computers store data in binary format, a series of bits that are either 0s or 1s. Numerical data is represented at the machine level as strings of bits. Numbers or letters are stored as 8 bits in a structure called a byte. In a big endian format, the most significant digit is the left-most byte (so the number is read left to right). In the little endian format, this is just the opposite, with the data read right to left. Operating systems such Windows NT are little endian; other operating systems such as HP-UX are big endian. It does not matter to the Itanium processor family architecture whether a system is little or big endian, because it is endian-agnostic and can work with both forms.

Explicit parallelism   An Itanium processor family compiler turns sequential code into parallelized 128-bit bundles of instructions that can be directly or explicitly parallel-processed by the CPU without having to interpret it further. *See* Implicit Parallelism *and* Compilers.

Explicitly Parallel Instruction Computing (EPIC)   EPIC is the acronym to describe the architecture behind the Itanium processor family architecture, co-developed by Hewlett-Packard and Intel. This design philosophy will eventually replace RISC and CISC.

Implicit parallelism (RISC)   A regular (non-Itanium processor family) compiler examines and optimizes sequential code for parallelism but then has to regenerate sequential code, relying on the processor to re-extract the parallelization as the instructions are executed by the CPU. The processor then has to read this implied parallelism from the machine code, rebuild it, and run it. The parallelism is there, but more decoding work has to be done by the hardware before it can be utilized. *See* Explicit Parallelism *and* Compilers.

Instruction set   The instructions list is assembly language used by the microprocessor. Traditionally, the two main instruction set philosophies were CISC, typified by IBM mainframes and Intel's Pentium processors, and RISC, typified by HP's PA-RISC processors and other vendors' RISC programs.

Itanium processor family   The Itanium processor family represents the entire range of processors that are based on the EPIC architecture, co-developed by HP and Intel.

Parallelism   For Itanium this refers to the ability to carry out many different tasks at once at the CPU or microprocessor level. Sequential events happen one after another; parallel events happen simultaneously. Modern RISC processor architectures have some capacity to do more than one operation at once. *See* Implicit parallelism *and* Explicit parallelism.

Processor   *See* Central processing unit (CPU)

Sequential   Events that execute one after are sequential. For example, all computer instructions are presented sequentially to the compiler. The execution of the program is optimized for the Itanium processor by finding blocks of the program that can be executed in parallel by the microprocessor.

Registers   A register is a temporary storage location within a processor where data can be stored for fast access. For example, when the processor needs to add two numbers, each number is stored in a register and the result of that addition is also stored. The Itanium processor family architecture specification specifies multiple sets of 64-bit registers.

Reduced Instruction Set Computer (RISC)   CISC processors predominantly used more complex instructions that required several clock cycles to execute, but did more work. RISC processors take a different approach by relying on shorter, simpler instructions that execute in one clock cycle so that more of them can be carried out per second. The HP PA-RISC processor uses RISC instructions.

Web Resources

Depending on the stage of your Itanium implementation and the role it plays within your organization, you may find yourself looking for more in-depth information.

The HP Itanium Home Page

http://www.hp.com/go/itanium

The HP Itanium Home Page is the ideal place to start. From here, you can navigate to more specific levels of information.

The DSPP Page

http://www.hp.com/dspp

The DSPP, or Developer and Solution Partner Portal, is the starting point for partners interested in the latest information about the HP–Intel alliance.

The Intel Itanium Home Page

http://www.intel.com/products/server/processors/server/itanium/

Intel's main page on Itanium is guaranteed to be stable, so if you are unable to find a different page listed on the *www.intel.com* site, this is the proper starting point. From this URL, information is available on

- Product information
- Processor performance
- Success stories

- Developer information
- Itanium-based server solutions
- Benefits of Itanium-based servers
- Benefits of Itanium-based workstations
- White papers
- Where to buy Itanium-based servers and workstations

Intel Itanium Processor Information

http://www.intel.com/products/server/processors/server/itanium/

Intel's own Itanium Home Page is a worthwhile place to look for information on the Itanium processor.

Intel Itanium Processor Information for Developers

http://developer.intel.com/design/itanium/index.htm?iid=search+Itanium&

This is a good starting point for developers; among other information, the Updated Itanium Architecture Software Developer's Manual is available here.

Intel Itanium Processor Information for Business

http://www.intel.com/eBusiness/products/itanium/index.htm?iid=search+Itanium&

If you are looking at Itanium from a business perspective as opposed to a developer's, this is the proper page to start reading. The latest business products and services are profiled at this URL.

Intel Itanium Processor Early Access Program

http://cedar.intel.com/cgi-bin/ids.dll/content/content.jsp?cnt-Key=Generic+Editorial::eap&cntType=IDS_EDITORIAL

Software developers will also want to gain more information about Intel's EAP, or Early Access Program, from this URL.

Intel Itanium Processor for Software Developers

http://cedar.intel.com/cgi-bin/ids.dll/topic.jsp?catCode=BMC

Developers can also access resources pertinent to their trade at this site.

Intel Itanium Processor Information

http://www.intel.com/products/server/processors/server/itanium/

Those looking for more technical information on the processor itself should start at this page.

Intel Itanium Processor Information for Developers

http://developer.intel.com/design/itanium/index.htm?iid=search+Itanium&

Similarly, if you are a developer and looking for more technical information on the processor itself, you should start at this page.

Intel Itanium Processor Information for Business

http://www.intel.com/eBusiness/products/itanium/index.htm?iid=search+Itanium&

Business-related service departments will find technical information on the processor itself at this URL.

APPENDIX C

Itanium Case Studies

Case Study 1: The University of Tennessee

Grid computing is one of the most exciting new frontiers in computational science; it will harness the power of diverse computer resources as never before. One institution at the forefront of grid computing research, the University of Tennessee, has set up a research grid to make this an attainable reality. Grid research may one day lead to huge distributed computing networks that will bring unimaginable compute power to bear on the biggest and most complex challenges in science, or allow every student fast access to supercomputing-type resources.

The University of Tennessee researchers constructed their grid to learn more about grid computing and to assess new high performance architectures that could be well suited to grid computing. They were particularly keen to test an HP workstation i2000 cluster equipped with Intel® Itanium™ processors which was made available through the Systems Grant program run jointly between HP and Intel that provides systems to world-class research institutions.

The University of Tennessee's Grid consists of seven clusters, until now a mixture of Sun servers and workstations and IA-32 workstations. Since September, a cluster of four Intel Itanium architecture workstations has been on the grid.

Director of the University of Tennessee's Innovative Computing Laboratory, Dr Jack Dongarra, explains: "The Intel Itanium processor family is an important architecture from Intel and we need to fully understand its capabilities. We're interested in developing software that runs in a portable way across a wide variety of architectures and, because of the potential importance of the Itanium processor in the future, we wanted to test it now as part of the grid.

"We believe it will be widely pervasive and so we wanted to get our software ported, tested, performance-optimized and ready for Itanium before it reaches market saturation. "

Portability is important for grid computing software, because a grid by definition should unite a variety of different architectures and operating environments into a cohesive computing resource. Therefore it is easiest and most efficient to be able to reuse code by being able to compile it on different architectures without having to rewrite or customize it.

Grid computing is a branch of computer science that is still in its infancy, but holds astounding potential to unite diverse compute resources as never before, forging together clustered desktop systems and the largest multiprocessor servers to create a virtual supercomputer that has the flexibility to handle a wide variety of differently sized tasks. Grids will bring terabytes of storage space and billions of compute cycles to bear on today's most taxing scientific problems.

But that is still off in the future and this vision will not be attainable without hard research work. Dr Dongarra states: "What we're interested in doing today is deploying a grid that's large enough to give us the ability to assess what we've done and how well it will work in a broader setting.

We're not trying to set up a fully mature computing center grid where users come to use lots of cycles. What drives us is the ability to do our research, to put in place ideas that find their way into the fabric of computing.

"We were thrilled when the opportunity came up for us to participate in HP and Intel's Itanium-based Systems Grant program and we were delighted when we heard that we received four HP workstation i2000 systems."

Early indications show the new architecture to be a powerful addition to the grid. Last September, 4 HP workstation i2000 systems were clustered together and went online as part of the Scalable Intracampus Research Grid (SInRG) project, which deploys a large grid infrastructure across a local area. The University of Tennessee's Knoxville's campus houses the entire project, which is geographically compact and efficient, making it easier to test communication structures and control mechanisms than in many other wide-area grid projects.

Dr Dongarra says: "We have a need to understand and explore the opportunities that the Intel Itanium architecture provides users. We are developing software for grid management, performance, measurement, and for scientific research. It is critical that this software is able to run across a variety of hardware platforms.

"Our users of the grid are running numerical software and they are accessing mathematical libraries we have developed to help solve some scientific computations, such as linear algebra. We also want to develop techniques for exploiting distributed heterogeneous computing. For either task, the Intel Itanium processor is a very powerful processor by today's standards."

The University of Tennessee created the original BLAS and LAPACK libraries that are widely used in scientific computing today. Linear algebra and vector math routines from these libraries are put to work across the world in a multitude of fields, from physics and astronomy to engineering, computer graphics, or biology.

Integrated easily, compiled quickly, runs stable

The SInRG grid, like all grids, needs "middleware" software that can integrate the parts into a coherent whole and manage the tasks from system to system and architecture to architecture.

NetSolve is the middleware that glues the clusters. It manages the mathematical and scientific tasks that users share across the grid by sending them to a cluster where they can be solved with the appropriate scientific or mathematical libraries, and then returns the results to the user's desktop.

NetSolve is a great example of the University of Tennessee's approach in making grid software highly portable and it is managing the SInRG grid today. It was developed in 1995 and is 64-bit clean so it can be compiled on any 64-bit architecture without the need to develop new code. It is intended to run 'out the box', and is built with standard Linux/UNIX tools.

Dr Dongarra says: "The NetSolve system was built on the Intel Itanium processor cluster with no trouble at all. Even though it was a new architecture, there was no need to make changes to our underlying software.

"Outside the standard UNIX/Linux components that came with Red Hat we didn't need anything. Once the software was compiled and linked, the Itanium cluster was up and on the grid within the day.

"We noticed the processing power of the Itanium processor right away when we started compiling our applications on it.

"We found it had a very fast compile time and our software build was done very quickly. When you've been using a last generation IA-32 or RISC processor and you have an expectation of how long it will take to compile your application, it is very impressive when you have a chance to put it on a very fast machine like the HP workstation i2000 and see how quickly it goes.

"The HP i2000s are very solid machines. The designs are very robust and they are very stable. We're very happy with the systems."

Parallelism and high performance

There are two key research groups involved in SInRG grid research: the middleware research group, and the interdisciplinary research group who are working on applications and optimizations to improve performance and open new areas of research. This latter group is particularly interested in parallelism in Grid computing.

Their research ranges from finding the best 'fine-grained' parallelism available with today and tomorrow's computer architectures for individual system and cluster performance, to studying ways of optimizing more 'coarse-grained' parallelism of networked data, message passing, and interconnect latencies. If these are optimized to keep pace with emerging technologies, then the strongest parallel performance can be attained across a grid.

Researchers at the University have installed their own math libraries and standards such as BLAS, and LAPACK for vector and linear algebra sets, common in scientific computing.

The next stage is to start figuring out how to extract highly-optimized performance. Jack Dongarra explains: "One thing that all of our applications people desire is the very fastest uniprocessor performance. When they have that, they'll start to work on parallel performance. Once they have assessed and optimized the performance on a single 1-way system, they look at optimizing dual processor performance. Then they look at how to optimize the cluster performance, then finally, the grid performance as a whole."

His own early benchmarking has shown a single HP workstation i2000 to have impressive performance in floating point intensive benchmarks.

He says: "Early performance testing on our HP workstation i2000 indicates that its performance in carrying out floating point operations was very impressive. It's a fresh architecture and it's already performing strongly."

HP systems based on the Intel Itanium processor family are ideal solutions for the rigors of scientific computing and grid deployment for four good reasons:

Excellent floating point performance, which is both fast and at a high level of precision—exactly what is needed for much computationally intensive scientific computing.

Its parallel architecture executes multiple instructions in a cascade rather than a linear path to get results back faster.

64-bits allows the use of more than 2GB of RAM, which is the maximum physical memory addressable by IA-32 architectures. The Itanium architecture can bring almost unlimited memory and address space resources to bear on the largest sets.

Today's 4.2GB/s peak main memory bus throughput keeps the processor fed with the data it needs, when it needs it to help process large computationally intensive sets quickly. Systems due in Q2 2002 have even more impressive bandwidth performance.

Furthermore, next generation systems can be expected to have unprecedented levels of price performance, ideal for universities and research groups where every dollar counts.

Academic problems solved with real world performance

Although its focus is research, the SInRG grid is not purely a computer science research tool—it is being tested in real-world situations every day. It is being used to solve scientific and mathematical challenges and as a learning tool for students from a number of departments on the University of Tennessee campus.

Departments at the University of Tennessee use the grid to solve their computational tasks, while at the same time doing their part to contribute in driving grid research forward. These include:

- Computational ecology—The Department of Ecology, and Evolutionary Biology uses the grid to run math sets for modeling, simulation, and data management. Computational ecology analyses and describes ecological systems and they run ecological simulation sets on the grid today. Sets like these help researchers to better understand the ecological web that surrounds us.
- Medical imaging—The UT Medical Center of Knoxville is using the SInRG Grid are leaders in the field of medical imaging. They run sets that help continued reseach into Positron Emission Tomography (PET), which helps us to monitor body organs function in real-time. Research run on the grid today may have valuable applications in tomorrow's medical diagnosis.
- Interactive Molecular Design—The UT Department of Chemistry uses SInRG to simulate the complex biochemical molecular interactions for visualization of molecules and chemical reactions. Itanium on the SInRG grid is helping us to understand the innermost functions of the cell.

Advanced Machine Design The UT Department of Electrical and Computer Engineering uses the Grid for ACS general purpose circuit simulator algorithm development, synthesis and evaluation. These teach students about the implementation of algorithms in gate arrays and help research into coding algorithms into hardware accelerator cards.

Dr Dongarra explains: "We are lucky to have a number of groups on campus who are willing to pioneer and explore these ideas along with us. They are willing to use the wide variety of resources and performance potential of our grid and so they are also helping to push back the frontiers of our research and their own research at the same time.

"We're thankful to have these enlightened colleagues to work with who help us in this way."

In the future, the SInRG grid has the potential to become an important node on the National Technology Grid, which is currently in planning between the Partnerships for Advanced Computational Infrastructure and a number of government agencies. Dr Dongarra hopes that some of the software and grid computing techniques researched on the SInRG grid in Tennessee will become integral parts of this awesome national effort.

He acknowledges that there is still a lot of work to do before grid computing becomes pervasive. "This notion of the grid in this heterogeneous way has been limited today to a research context and has not yet found its way into the fabric of scientific computing in general. However, because of grid computing's ability to deliver the best computing performance to the widest audience, it is only a matter of time.

"There is much to be done to provide the tools and to educate people on how grid computing can be used to benefit everyone. The challenge is overcoming network speed limitations. In the near term as bandwidth issues get addressed by developing technology, the face of distributed network computing will change dramatically. As the network speeds get faster, the limitation will move back to the power of the computing platform installed on the grid. If the network itself is as fast as the computer's internal links, then having extreme performance architectures such as the Intel Itanium architecture becomes even more critical.

"This notion of using geographically distributed resources will become more of a reality and this idea of grid-based computing will become more natural to a wider group of people."

He also sees a bright future for the Intel Itanium architecture in grid and high-performance computing: "I would expect that in the future that the Intel Itanium architecture will be the architecture that people purchase. People talk about Pentium now; tomorrow it will be the Intel Itanium processor family.

"We want to have a good understanding of what those processors are capable of so that when that happens we can have our software ready to go and have it run at a very high level of performance.

"It is fair to say that Intel Itanium architecture systems offer scientists the ability to streamline their research and test larger and more complex sets than ever before. It is likely that the Intel Itanium processor family will play an integral part in both large and small discoveries of tomorrow's science and will improve the productivity among researchers, scientists, and faculty today."

Case Study 2: Sony Pictures Imageworks

Sony Pictures Imageworks has had a lion's share of the recent big budget visual effects movies.

If you are a regular moviegoer, the list of titles that the digital production company has worked on will be very familiar; *Harry Potter and the Sorcerer's Stone*, *Cast Away*, *Charlie's Angels*, *Hollow Man*, *Contact*, *Godzilla* and *Starship Troopers*, not to mention the upcoming and highly anticipated *Spider-Man*, *Stuart Little 2* and

Charlie's Angels 2. Imageworks will also embark on its first all Computer Graphics film, *AstroBoy*, in 2002.

These productions push the limits of visual effects techniques and test the limits of today's computer technologies. Sony Picture Imageworks works hard to stay on top of the technology curve to ensure it can continue to bring the latest jaw-dropping effects to movie screens around the world.

The company has some of the finest artists in the business, and they require tools that can keep pace with their vision for the visual effects of tomorrow. That's why Sony Pictures Imageworks elected to evaluate Intel® Itanium™ processor workstations from Hewlett-Packard.

Today's audiences demand better, more astounding effects. Each movie frame must have more and more detail. From a technology standpoint the sheer volume of data that defines a single frame of the next blockbuster movie can be equal to the amount of information in one copy of the Encyclopaedia Britannica. There are 24 frames in every second of movie. Multiply this by the number of seconds in a minute and the number of minutes in a movie and you can begin to see how tremendously complex it has become to make a visual effects movie.

And it doesn't stop there. Tomorrow's movies will be higher in resolution than the movies of today. The sheer amount of data involved can test 32-bit workstation architectures.

The IA-32 specification only allows a maximum of 2GB of physical memory. This means that in the animation process for sets over that limit, resources must be focused on optimizing the sets to fit into the available memory space. Remove this limit and the artists would easily be able to work with longer, more detailed animations. In rendering, the processors would be able to address many gigabytes of RAM for faster rendering of more complex scenes.

A senior engineer in Sony Picture Imageworks' software department, Evan Smyth, describes the challenge he and the animators face: "Entire datasets required to get the visual effects of today and tomorrow are going above 2GB. An entire scene and all the data that's going into it, including the lighting and that sort of thing, can easily go over 2GB.

"Since a 32-bit architecture can handle a limited amount of physical memory, everyone in the industry who works on 32-bit workstations has to work in a different way. Those of us who are building the most challenging visual effects will also be spending time optimizing for this limit, or working with lower resolution models when we're animating. It's part of the production process.

"In a 64-bit future, we could work with higher-resolution models, and we could dispense with the necessity of developing optimizations for 32-bit architectures. Itanium has the headroom we need in memory addressability and the performance to do this so we can work on a newer generation of visual effects."

Bruce Dobrin is a Senior Engineer from systems R&D. He has had the same experience: "We are continuing to exceed the hard 2GB limit for a processes we are running today. There are ways we have developed that allow us to work around that issue but the optimum solution is to provide platforms that could access more than 2GB of memory. Then we could spend less time optimizing and focus all our efforts instead on creating newer effects that will challenge your next generation Itanium processors. We believe that 64-bit computing will be very important."

"Alias|Wavefront's Maya is our primary interactive desktop around here, so we tested that first. It performed well on the HP workstation i2000 and the workstation was extremely stable. Our initial tests of Maya were considered successful. We believe that Itanium will be an important platform for Sony Pictures Imageworks in the longer-term."

Sony Pictures Imageworks tested modeling and animation performance on Maya. Other tasks that Sony Pictures Imageworks is considering the Itanium processor family for include rendering and compositing. The company currently has a 1000 processor render farm, divided between 600 IA-32 systems and 300 SGI UNIX systems.

The Explicitly Parallel Instruction Computing (EPIC) architecture in the Itanium processor family combines a number of powerful software and hardware refinements that accelerate floating point performance, memory throughput, and parallel performance. The net result is an architecture that today can work on six instructions per clock cycle. This combination of speed and parallelism translates into powerful performance benefits for companies like Sony Pictures Imageworks.

It means that the Itanium processor can do more in less time than its competitive 64-bit architectures, and it has greater scalability than its 32-bit counterparts.

Furthermore, Intel's expertise in processor manufacturing means that it has leading 64-bit price/performance today, and is likely to extend that lead tomorrow.

Amit Agrawal heads up the Software Department for Sony Pictures Imageworks. He is interested in deploying Itanium processor-based systems into the render farm: "One place that we have also run into limitations with memory addressibility is in rendering, which is also floating point intensive. Rendering is an obvious task that could benefit from 64-bit performance, but price-performance is highly important for a node in a render farm. Since we expect the Itanium processor family to give us the best bang for the buck in price performance, rendering will be a task we will begin early with the Itanium processor family.

"Near real-time high-speed compositing would also be another important area in which the Itanium processor family will excel, largely thanks to its multimedia instruction set and its wide memory bandwidth."

Compositing is a technique in which two or more images that are created separately are layered over the top of each other to create a single image. The layers are made of millions of 32 bit pixels that are combined mathematically to create a seamless picture. In a movie-quality composited image, there should be no indication that the image was ever separated. Like rendering, it is highly processor and bandwidth intensive.

Sony Pictures Imageworks has a list of 3rd party applications that they would like to see ready for the deployment on the Itanium processor family, including Maya, RenderMan, Discreet's Inferno, Side Effects Software's Houdini, and Adobe Photoshop. Some of these applications, like Houdini, are already available on the Itanium architecture, others are in the process of being ported.

Itanium is ideal for the entertainment industry

The Itanium processor family architecture is able to rise to the challenge of such tasks, offering a number of benefits to the entertainment industry, including:

* 64-bit addressibility to allow the memory scalability and addressability for the future.
* superior floating point performance for continuing performance improvements in the fields of animation and rendering.
* high level of parallelism for fast throughput of highly complex computations and image data sets.

Today's 32-bit processors allow a maximum of 2GB of physical memory, but the HP workstation i2000 can be loaded with 16GB or more of RAM. The extra capacity afforded by 64 bit systems' architecture is greater than that of 32 bit systems by a factor of 4 billion.

Floating point performance is critical to many digital content creation applications specifically used in modeling, animating, and rendering.

The EPIC architecture does not disappoint. It allows two 32-bit numbers to be worked on simultaneously in parallel. Its 128 80-bit floating point registers provide highly precise and fast floating point calculations, useful in complex physics engines and ray-tracing calculations. This sort of power is needed in providing realistic dynamic physics in animations, and also photorealistic renders. Rotating floating point registers allow many floating point loop iterations to run in parallel enabling more efficient execution.

The floating point performance of the HP workstation i2000 today is industry leading, according to results from the independent benchmarking organization SPEC.

All these features will be pressed into service in the future. Amit Agrawal explains: "In the past, image files used to be the limiting factor in defining our storage requirements. Lately we've been experiencing a trend where the data that goes into generating the image files is getting larger and larger. Final image files are now a constant size that is not increasing—for a movie it's about 1.5TB. But the data that goes into creating that movie is increasing at an extraordinary rate. We believe that the Itanium processor family has the potential to help us meet this challenge.

"Our audiences like to see complexity in some fashion in visual effects on the screen. This complexity can come in the form of an army of characters or in the form of finer, subtle details like the interactions of hair or feathers. To achieve this photorealism, we are always able to find ways of increasing the data set size, and that's the trend I see."

EPIC is an architecture that has been built to handle complex data in large amounts. It has the memory bandwidth to provide wide channels for the data to flow through. It has powerful floating point and multimedia units that can carry out large calculations to a high precision in parallel. It will be able to address more than 4GB of memory and it has astounding future potential, as the architecture has a theoretical address limit of 18 billion gigabytes of memory.

As Sony Pictures Imageworks continues its leadership in the digital visual effects industry, the company's data set sizes will certainly continue to grow. It will be the workstations developed around the Itanium processor family that will meet the challenge.

Case Study 3: NCAC

The NCAC came into being in 1992 with a joint contract between the Federal Highway Administration and the National Highway Traffic Safety Administration. Affiliated with the George Washington University in Virginia, NCAC is part of the School of Engineering and Applied Science at the George Washington University, and shares its data—including over 14,000 crash test films that can be ordered online—with interested parties worldwide.

The NCAC first partnered with Hewlett-Packard Company in 1996, after receiving a joint research grant from American Automotive Manufacturers Association and the US Department of Transportation to evaluate the current state-of-the-art parallel computers running crash computing software.

"It was during this evaluation that we first started working with HP," explained Kan. "Back then we were also looking at Cray, IBM and Silicon Graphics. Since then, we have developed a strong technology partnership with HP. As such, we have evaluated all of HP's high-end platforms, starting with the HP 9000 V-Class Enterprise Servers, and finally to HP's new Itanium™ - based system."

With simulated modeling analysis performed by the FHWA/NHTSA National Crash Analysis Center at the George Washington University, it's no surprise to see weighty reports with such heady titles as:

• "Crash Exposure and Crashworthiness of Sport Utility Vehicles."

- "Injury Patterns Among Belted Drivers Protected by Air Bags in 30 to 35 mph Crashes."
- "Chest Injury Risks to Drivers for Alternative Air Bag Inflation Rates."

These are but a few of the hundreds of vehicle crash test analysis reports that come out of the NCAC film library—tests that are performed with the expressed purpose of saving the lives of drivers and passengers.

According to Cing-Dao "Steve" Kan, Director of Simulation and Modeling Research at the NCAC, "We typically perform complex computer simulation of vehicle impact—including car to car crashes—many times over in conjunction with the Department of Transportation and leaders in the automotive industry, such as Ford, Chrysler and GM."

He continued, "In the past we have developed detailed computer models for the assessment of the crash-worthiness of vehicles, all of which require an immense amount of computational power. As the modeling analysis becomes more complex, the need for a high-end supercomputer is essential."

Kan states that, "The recently installed 4-Way HP rx4610 Itanium®-based Server was up and running within a week of delivery—and there was absolutely no learning curve to deal with. As far as we were concerned, it was just another HP-UX system."

The introduction of Itanium™-based servers marks a new chapter in enterprise-class computing. It establishes a solid foundation designed to deliver the performance, innovation and price to customers like NCAC.

Co-developed with Intel, the 4-Way HP rx4610 that NCAC installed is one of three Itanium™-based systems utilizing the Intel® Itanium™ Instruction Set Architecture that was co-developed by HP. Also available are the HP-UX, a 64-bit UNIX operating system, is optimized for the Itanium™-based architecture to provide the performance, scalability and reliability NCAC has come to expect from the HP-UX operating environment.

"We started running several large modeling programs immediately," Kan confirmed. "Our compact-sized vehicle program has about 300,000 element models within it—the industry standard size of program for benchmarking—with 1.8 million degrees of freedom." With their tests to date, NCAC has determined that the HP rx4610 server is four times faster than the V-Class, per CPU. As Kan explained, "In terms of bus speed the V-Class has around 200Mhz, and the rx4610 has 775Mhz—again four times as fast. When we're running the UNIX applications, it's definitely four times faster than the V-Class, and against the Silicon Graphics 2000, the Itanium™-based system is about three times faster."

NCAC will continually run several different types of jobs at one time to analyze performance across various types of software, and to confirm that the programs all run as expected on the parallel platform.

Kan noted, "We run tests with DSMP, MTP, MPI and also message passing, starting with one CPU, then adding another one by one, just to see how the scalability compares with the other platforms we've tested. The test results with the rx4610 have been beyond my expectations."

According to Kan, a typical crash event—such as a car crashing into a wall—occurs within 150 milliseconds. He's happy to confirm that "now we can run the software to see what happens when a car runs into a highway barrier and gets bounced back onto the highway. This whole event would take 2-3 seconds, a simulation that is much longer in duration. The CPU cycles are much more intensive, which is why we want to see how the parallel performance behaves."

Software and support services

NCAC is currently using LS/DYNA software. HP partners with MDA software vendors to optimize their programs for HP platforms. This partnership means that designers using HP systems have the application performance to evaluate more design options and do more accurate analysis.

Kan concluded, "We've found the support team at HP to be very helpful as well. They assisted with the set-up and having direct access to the performance specialists in Dallas has been most gratifying. We also worked with the group of consultants that are porting LS/DYNA and assisted in creating the executable code, allowing us to compare our performance results with HP's."

Fast forward your business with HP Itanium-based services now: **http:// www.hp.com/go/itanium**

Case Study 4: Datev Eg

Itanium solution excites leading european tax association

Datev eG is Germany's largest association of self-employed tax consultants, auditors and lawyers with a membership of 38,000 that represents about 65% of the German market in this sector.

As a cooperative organisation, it provides vital electronic data processing (EDP), software and organisational services to its members who act for more than two million clients in Germany.

Its services include such things as database management, payroll, tax computation, financial accounting and data analysis.

Common Platform

Beside their MVS based data processing Datev also provides a growing number of services from UNIX, NT and Linux environments and it realised that placing these on a common platform could increase efficiency and cut costs. They saw a possible answer in the next generation computing technology offered by the Itanium processor family, co-developed by Hewlett-Packard and Intel and capable of supporting HP-UX, Microsoft Windows NT and Linux.

"We hold information on UNIX and NT systems for all kinds of purposes from internal file and print applications to external Web services," said Datev's UNIX System Manager, Juergen Haeusinger. "We have HP-UX database services for such things as company archives and information systems e.g., for jurisdiction,and we also have a still small number of Linux applications."

Pilot Project

"Since we have had a long association with HP, we discussed this and decided that we would co-operate with them in an Itanium pilot project."

For the pilot, a four processor Itanium platform has been installed at Datev. HP-UX Oracle databases and some of Datev's own database programs have been transferred to it, and Datev also plans to conduct some Web server tests on the new system.

The pilot will help Datev in adjusting the further strategy concerning their non-mainframe computing technologies. It will also assist HP in offering its customers a common, scalable and unique platform on which they can run a variety of operating systems.

Good Performance

Only part-way through the pilot project, the Itanium system is already proving a success at Datev.

"Because we will have less of a variety of systems, we will have less cost of ownership and cost of management so it will enable us to fulfil the needs of our customers more cost effectively and more efficiently."

"We have had a long association with HP and since they are very involved in the development of the Itanium system, they are the right partner for us concerning the pilot project."

Case Study 5: Penoles

An Alliance That Is Worth Its Weight in Silver

For 20 years, Grupo Peñoles has turned to HP, on one hand to have the industry-leader as a technical ally and, on the other hand, to reduce costs and enhance processes. Currently, all the Company's concerns have been transformed into leadership opportunities.

When Grupo Peñoles, global leader in silver production, considered the fact of reducing production costs, the thought did not take long to transform into action. With a relationship of more than 20 years, Peñoles and HP have jointly worked to maintain the Mexican mining giant in a technological state-of-art through different computing periods, from the mini-computer era and the first PCs, to the client-server concept and a variety of processes which shaped the technical process control solutions.

But upgrading is a constant and relentless job. This is why Peñoles needed to implement a technological renovation plan, which could allow constant equipment upgrade and operational cost optimization.

The need to have high-performance servers to optimize processes and costs led the mining company to consider installing the best available microprocessor in their equipment.

With this measure, Peñoles' technical staff performed long evaluations with Alpha processors (development of the ancient *Digital*) and Sparc (manufactured by Sun Microsystems), as well as with the "antique" 32-bit Intel and the new and powerful Itanium, HP and Intel's most recent development.

A Great Challenge

Peñoles' necessity to find the best price-benefit relationship to choose the perfect technology is not a whim. The fact of maintaining low costs is due to the fact that the international markets control the prices of metals in the mining industry. "There is no way to manage them, the only option we have to compete is reducing operational costs, which has been one of our main strategies. If we do not have a project to optimize our costs, we are dead," said Mario Antonio Gonzalez Negrete, Peñoles's Computing manager.

For this reason, as a matter of survival, Peñoles must maintain competitive costs in a global level. "During the current recession, we experienced a reduction in metal prices, thus, a lot of mining companies disappeared," said Gonzalez Negrete. This is a cyclic business; if we do not reach the leadership in cost-optimization, we can disappear, and the key formula to obtain cost-optimization is the technological innovation."

The challenge of HP was enormous in order to support an enterprise that cannot hesitate on its decisions. HP not only had to help reducing costs, but also had to develop a process for the equipment's good operation in critical conditions, as extraction mines and the adverse environment in which they operate.

"The reliability of the equipment in difficult underground circumstances, where dust and meteorological conditions are extreme, was another factor in our election," said Francisco Javier Rabago Garcia, inner consultant of this mining enterprise. "We tried other equipment, but all of them failed. HP's equipment is the only one that proved being resistant enough."

With such premises, one of the first steps taken to help Peñoles was the establishment of an equipment upgrade program. "The renovation of the equipment each two or three years allow us to deploy state-of-art technology all the time," said Mario Antonio Gonzalez Negrete. "The Company's upgrade with an attractive profitability plan means a lot to us. Besides the fact of seeking all technical options in the market, we have optimized our equipment, support and maintenance costs."

HP's applications were applied in different areas of the mining enterprise -- from the initial mineral extraction processes on different mines, to management aspects in offices located in all the country. "Being close to an enterprise that supports us and teaches us in all the aspects related to technology, is a strategic and a very important element for our cost optimization project," said Gonzalez Negrete.

Currently, Peñoles has 2,500 HP personal computers and more than 100 HP servers in all the country, as well as workstations for specific technical solutions.

The King Itanium

As its upgrade challenge, this mining enterprise had as a goal the fact of running management, technical measurement and production control processes, all in the same computer.

In this aspect, the *benchmark* results were definite. "When given a *find* command in a 7,200-revolution disk, it took between 40 and 60 seconds to find something with a 32-bit technology. With Itanium, this same research is performed in just three seconds! Another important aspect is that: it is 60% cheaper equipment than the one that the competition offers," said Pedro Luis Sanchez Armas, Grupo Peñoles' Software Research Manager. Besides its high performance, the king Itanium offers a low cost computing network operation.

"We choose the Itanium technology because it offers us a high development at a low cost," said Sanchez Armas. "The first ten 4610 Itanium servers are already operating and further equipment is on its way in order to perform a higher quantity of research in our workstation."

"Having a technologic upgrade agreement with HP allows us to have higher performance technology at a lower cost, where productivity grows with higher capacity and information flow ease of use," said Sanchez Armas.

"We have always being searchers of new technologies, and we always have been supported by HP in this process. We consider ourselves as pioneers, not because we want to be so, but because we want to be the best. We knew there was a 64- bit technology 8 or 9 years ago, but we believe that this technology has reached its maturing point—not only the hardware, but also the software that has the capacity of leveraging that hardware," said Sanchez Armas.

Due to the implementation of Itanium microprocessors in 10 of its servers under Linux and HP-UX operating systems, Peñoles performs all the functions it always wanted to perform, "but we are looking forward to obtaining more through the software that will be developing for this processor, and I believe that we will soon obtain it," proudly said Gonzalez Negrete.

For Peñoles, the Linux-HP combination was considered as a productivity detonator. With Linux, the company already celebrated four years developing its own firewalls, as well as its mails and web services.

The plan is to integrate Itanium into all the solutions and thus reduce even more IT and process costs, integrating the applications on a single type of processor.

Working in Tough Conditions

HP's equipment is deployed in difficult access places, i.e. mining units, to perform geology and reserve calculation solutions; in process control, connected with real-time equipment; or in management aspects, including e-business.

The Itanium processor will run all the applications developed by the mining company. One of them is Promin, which will run the preventive and the corrective maintenance of the production facilities and all the new generated aspects.

In order to maintain low costs, all management systems receive maintenance information in order to see the deployment of the equipment (mills, motors, breakers, etc.) and receive direct information of the process control: quantity of material already processed, kilowatts per hour consumed by the facility, etc. All this information is needed in order to have a production support database.

"We have all the information located in one place; this way we have access to what is happening in the extraction and the mineral recuperation processes. Another benefit is that we have reduced the volume of used consumables," said the Computing manager.

"Where else have we had more positive results?" asked Rabago Garcia, "Definitely in e-business. We are running the security system in order to eliminate the fact of being invaded by people that could enter to the e-business systems. Added to the reliance that we have to the HP's hardware."

Talking about e-business, Peñoles has two very important selling points. The first one is Quadrem, a market place formed by the most important mining businesses in the world, where machines, equipment, and services are commercialized.

The other one is the creation of a Grupo Bal market place (Industrias Peñoles, Grupo Palacio de Hierro, Grupo Nacional Provincial, Valores Mexicanos Casa de Bolsa y Credito Afianzador), where all providers of all the horizontal lines will be displayed. Currently some products have been catalogued, performing supply agreements with vendors. This will begin during the first quarter of the year 2002.

With these market places, the acquisition cycle getting smaller. "This is the first step," said Rabago Garcia. "With this, the inventory is reduced and if we have useless equipment, and it can be offered to a provider and sold to those who really need it."

Through these actions, Peñoles has improved its productivity up to 60%, and also has reduced its production costs. In the acquisition process, for example, all the procedures that were performed in two weeks are currently performed in two days.

This way, Peñoles not only can survive to the metal market changes, but also can lead this sector world-wide through an alliance with HP, which is worth its weigh in silver. The Company will also contribute by maintaining its position as the main producer of this metal in the world.

Index